"*Winter Has Passed* is a life
that our God is a living Go
collection of God stories. I
fresh ways, igniting long-lo
reminded me of the One who speaks to dry bones and calls
them to life. May He do the same for you!"

Laura Jacob, Adjunct Professor
Life Pacific College, San Dimas, CA

"Diana Greene combines personal stories, passion for prayer,
and practical prayer applications in a way that encourages me
to talk with my loving Heavenly Father."

Pastor John E. Baker
Grace Church, Molalla OR

"This book sure packs a punch of truth. It filled me to
overflowing with anticipation for what God is going to do
next as we come out of the "winter" of our lives. Diana has
the ability to tell through everyday stories how God works in
individual lives of those willing to listen to Him and obey. Sit
down and read with the expectation that God will speak to you
through *Winter Has Passed*."

Mark Hazen, Associate Pastor
Grace Church, Molalla, OR

"God used *Winter Has Passed* to lavish the hope of God's
sovereignty onto the story and situations I am in the midst
of now. Diana's book will have you hungry to listen for God's
gentle whispers of spring in your own personal stories and
reflecting on His intimate involvement in the details of your
life."

Sue Hazen, Office Manager, Pastor's wife

Winter Has Passed

Sarah,

May your winters
be short & your
springs long

Diana

Come now, My love.
My lovely one, come.

For you, the winter has passed,
the snows are over and gone,
the flowers appear in the land,
the season of joyful songs has come.

The cooing of the turtledove
is heard in our land.

Come now, My love.
My lovely one, come.

Let Me see your face
and let Me hear your voice,
For your voice is sweet
and your face is beautiful.

Come now, My love.
My lovely one, come.

Song of Songs 2:10-14
received June 5, 2009

Winter Has Passed

Finding the Extraordinary in the Ordinary

Diana E. Greene

Diana Greene Ministries, LLC

Published by Diana Greene Ministries, LLC
PO Box 902, Molalla, OR 97038 www.DianaGreeneMinistries.com

Library of Congress Cataloging-in-Publication Data

Greene, Diana E.
Winter has passed, finding the extraordinary in the ordinary /by Diana E. Greene

ISBN - 13: 978-0-9895510-2-1
ISBN - 10: 0989551024

1. Christian Living 2. Inspirational 3. Prayer–Christian 4. Holy Spirit

Printed in the United States of America

Dedication

To My Husband, John

*In good times and in bad times,
I will always love you.*

Contents

Foreword

I so admire Diana's heart for helping people find their wholeness in the LORD. She has had a long season of personal ministry that is now expanding into publication. *Undivided Heart*, Diana's first two-part book, gave us a tool for healing that has helped so many people come to wholeness of heart, mind, spirit, and soul.

The stories in *Winter Has Passed* touch one from a different side. These are not just heart warming stories – though they certainly are that – but are narrative lessons from God. They gain access to the depths of one's heart and mind and spirit to enable pondering at deepest levels. These profoundly personal stories are combined with reflections, challenges, and passages for further study.

If you want inspiration, watch the Hallmark Channel. If you want your life with the Lord transformed, renewed, and enriched, then feast on these stories. But be warned: like the parables of Jesus, they are layered and subversive. They will cause you to look at yourself and your relationship with the Lord again and again, peeling off layers and becoming vulnerable to the work of His Spirit.

Gerry Breshears, PhD
Professor of Theology
Western Seminary, Portland, OR

Preface

A spiritual director once asked me, "Why did you write
Undivided Heart, Book One and Book Two? What is the
story behind this book which contains tools to help others
become unstuck emotionally, physically and spiritually?"

"Good question," I thought. As I shared personal stories
that brought about the lessons in my *Undivided Heart* books,
I realized the work that took twenty-seven years to develop
was born out of my own intimate journey with God.
Following that discussion, I decided to share these stories of
spiritual struggle and life learning.

This is how *Where is the Water?*, the first book in my
series *Finding the Extraordinary in the Ordinary*, was born.
Winter Has Passed is the second book in this series, and
though the works stand alone, they both speak to my belief
that prayer is an unceasing and intimate communication
with God.

The discipline of prayer has been a life-long quest. Many
hours spent alone with the Lord brought a desire to be close
to him throughout the day. I was dissatisfied with an hour
of prayer in the morning, so I found additional Bible study
and reading time in the afternoon. But I found this to be
inadequate. I wanted to spend all day with God. However, I
was a full-time mother and a working wife. Was it possible?

The Lord showed me that he is as close as the air I
breathe, involved in the most minute details of my daily
life. He would help me become aware of him and discover
lessons of truth in the middle of mundane tasks. What I
needed to do was embrace the life he called me to and find

him in the center of it.

Intimacy with God requires continual surrender of my expectations, letting go of "my rights" and the way I believe things ought to be. It also requires disciplined times of reading Scripture, praying, and reflecting back to see where God was in each day. I have discovered faith requires wrestling with doubt, fear, and having the courage to risk looking like a fool for God.

Within each personal story of *Winter Has Passed* is an example of how I have learned these disciplines. In the **Reflection**, I share what I learned from each story. In the **Challenge**, I invite you to discern how you can learn from similar experiences in your own life. Finally, Scripture references provide you with **Further Study** on the topics presented in the story.

My hope is that you will find the winters of your life, the hard and unexpected times, can be transformed into seasons of joy when you focus on intimate company with God.

> *"Delight yourself in the LORD; and He will give you the desires of your heart."*   PSALM 37:4 (NAS)

> *"Watch over your heart with all diligence, for from it flow the springs of life."*   PROVERBS 4:23 (NAS)

Diana E. Greene
Molalla, OR
Fall 2013

In Appreciation

The Lord continues to bless me with the skills of a young woman who has matured way beyond her years. Amanda (Halvorson) Greene, I praise the Lord for your spiritual insight, encouragement, editing skills, humor and personal care which have made this project come together.

By working together on this book, I was able to get to know the depth of the woman my son married. It has been a great honor to share insights, and I look forward to working on many more projects together. Thank you for believing in what the Lord had given me to do and for coming along side me to accomplish it.

No project can move forward without the diligence of those behind the scenes. John Greene, thank you for consistently encouraging me to "keep going, stay focused on the goal and the Lord." Without your willingness to support my efforts, this book would never have been completed.

David Wallace, thank you for continuing to be my tech support. I appreciate your extensive knowledge and generosity in sharing your expertise.

Mike Palmer, once again you offer your photography talent. I appreciate your eye for beauty and your expertise in catching God's creation. Your generous heart in sharing your fantastic photos is so appreciated.

Sue Hazen, thank you for agreeing to proof read the draft of the draft. I appreciate your time and talents given to this project.

When we needed an expert eye to catch any detail we may have missed, Laura Jacob, you freely offered your talent. Thank you for being so generous with your time and editing skills. Your eye for the big picture was needed and appreciated.

Thank you Gerry Breshears, Bev Hislop, Leslie Nelson, Mark Hazen, Sue Hazen, Laura Jacob, and John Baker. In the midst of VERY busy schedules, you took the time to read, comment, and encourage us. I thank each of you for your endorsement.

Jeremy Carman, [jalopyhead.com] thank you for your continued help with advertising and your excellent web design. I appreciate all the behind the scenes work you do to keep us up and running.

Luke Greene, thank you for your input. I know that with your wife fully involved you created time to check stories for accuracy, readability, and detail. Thank you also for letting me share how the boy I knew has grown into a compassionate man of God.

Nathan Greene, thank you for agreeing to do the final proof reading of this book despite a demanding schedule. Thank you also for letting me share your early years.

Gail Watson, thank you for sharing your expertise in preparing this book for publication. Your willingness to go the extra mile, to try new things and to share your talent make this project a joy.

Thank you to all who prayed for this book: Ruth, Marcia, Denise, Mom, Sue, Julie, Vance, Paula, Claire, John B., the Grace Church Women's Bible Study group. Your prayers and encouragement as we drafted, edited and worked against other deadlines were appreciated.

We serve an awesome God. I am grateful for his vision, faithfulness to complete the work, and the inspiration he provides. I am thankful that he answers prayers in ways I do not expect. Life with him is an adventure.

May the Holy Spirit continue to flow through my life and the lives of those who surrender to him. And may you, the reader, be blessed with an undivided heart that learns to pray expecting the unexpected.

Introduction

Mystery; it is a style of books and movies that we enjoy, but when it is a part of our own lives, we become frustrated. We like to feel we are in control. We want to know how our lives are going to play out. But many of life's events cannot be anticipated or controlled. How do we respond when we encounter the unexpected, like finding a white lily blooming in winter snow?

We want God to interact with us in our mundane moments and to share with Him our desires and needs. But we want Him to respond in ways we can predict.

What if He answers in a way we don't expect? What if His answer requires us to do something we are not comfortable with? Will we have the courage to obey and follow through?

In this second book of *Finding the Extraordinary in the Ordinary* series, Diana explores moments when she asked herself these same questions. In these times, she had to choose not only to listen but also to surrender to the way God wanted to answer prayers.

Winter Has Passed depicts common experiences from the workplace, the home, and even a doctor's office. In these stories, Diana honestly shares when she struggled to believe, argued with God, and, most importantly, when she chose to obey even when it did not make sense.

Society tells us to be independent and in control. But God gives us opportunities to do the opposite: become dependent on Him and give Him control.

A dependent lifestyle of surrender, of listening and obeying, is never easy. But God can turn our sorrows into joys and our winters into springs—not in spite of—but in the midst of our daily events.

I hope the stories in *Winter Has Passed* encourage and challenge you to be open to the unexpected and extraordinary ways God wants to interact with you.

Amanda Greene
Editor in Chief
a_greene@outlook.com

I Got Fired!

"I got fired!"

"What do you mean, 'You got fired'?" My husband, John, took the letter from my hand and started reading it.

Then, as if talking to himself, "You got fired. I can't believe it."

"I guess she didn't like me going to her boss," I told him. "She didn't come in until 9 am, and then she went promptly out to breakfast, came back for a couple of hours, took a long lunch, because how could she get her shopping done! Then she had the nerve to leave early!"

My frustration was obvious. As a secretary for the human resources department in the early 70's, I had been covering for my boss's lack of interest in her work. When she asked me to interview people for the various departments, I was flattered and excited to do it.

But one of the other department heads confronted me. She told me she did not like my choices in applicants. I was furious. The woman applicant I chose was almost over-qualified. She was the best fit for the job. That was not the problem. The problem, the department head made clear, when she got into my face and yelled:

"If you ever send me a Black again, I'll see that you regret it!" Then she turned and stomped back upstairs.

1

I was angry. *I had hired the perfect person!*

I could not play this political game. My boss needed to do her own job. I was no longer going to work hard and receive no compensation.

When I went to the President of the company about my boss's hours, he said, "I'll look into it."

A lot of good it did me. John and I went to Mexico for vacation, and when we came back, I was fired!

The temp agency told me not to fight it. They would find me another job. Within a couple of weeks, they made good on their promise.

Three months later they called me at my new job:

"Guess what?"

"What?"

"She's been fired."

"What?"

"The President fired her two months ago. I guess he discovered you were telling the truth."

"You're kidding."

"No, and she is working in your building."

"What?"

"I got her a job working in the other tower. I wanted you to know in case you run into her."

I hung up the phone. I couldn't believe it. I was in charge of eight floors of equipment and the receptionists for each floor. I went into my boss's office with an idea.

"I just learned that my old boss is working in the other

tower. I guess they found out I was telling the truth."

"Really?"

"Yes, and the agency told me she is getting a divorce."

"Oh, that's too bad." I knew he would feel that way.

"I was wondering…would it be alright with you if I went down and bought red roses and had one of the receptionists take them up to her?"

"You feel bad for her?"

"Well, she's had a rough time of it."

"Sure. Go ahead."

About 30 minutes after the receptionist delivered the flowers, I got a call.

"Hey, can you meet for coffee?" It was my old boss.

When I spotted her sitting at a small round table in the corner of the cafe, she looked thin and worn out. As I settled myself into a chair, she began:

"Thanks for the flowers."

I nodded in response.

"How did you find out?" she was referring to my note that came with the flowers telling her I was sorry to hear about her divorce.

"The temp agency told me."

She took a deep breathe. "I'm sorry."

"Sorry for what?"

She looked at me like, "You know what."

"When you went on vacation, I hired a temp," she

3

explained. "But before she got there, I refiled the folders in your desk drawer and in the file cabinet. When I asked the temp for a file, of course, she could not find it. I had no trouble getting her to back me up that you were incompetent and unable to handle the job."

I was wondering how she came up with the lies that lead to my dismissal.

I could see the anguish on her face. "Hey, don't worry about it."

"I'm sorry." She looked sincere.

"It has all worked out for the best," I assured her.

"What do you mean?" she asked.

"I would never have left that place, even though I hated working there."

She smiled at me.

"No," I started to explain, "not because of you. There was so much political garbage going on—things that I just didn't want to be a part of."

She knew I was referring to their hiring practices that did not follow the law.

"Besides," I continued, "I am making $600 more a month now. It would have taken me forever to get that pay raise!"

She laughed. "So you're OK then."

"Yes; the Lord answered my prayer. I got out of there, got a better paying job, I love the people I am working with and ..." I broke out in a big grin, "I love my boss."

She smiled at me. I had spent many afternoons listening

to her troubles. She tested the waters and realized I was open, so she proceeded to tell me what happened between her and her husband.

When I returned to work, my boss asked me:

"So how did it go?"

"She'll be OK."

"Did she like the flowers?"

"Loved them! Thanks."

"Sure. I left letters on your desk to type." He smiled like, "Glad it all worked out."

REFLECTION

We never know what troubles someone is going through. We judge them by their behavior without looking beyond the obvious.

At first, I felt I was fired for integrity reasons—because I had some. But in the end, I realized the deeper, unexpected lesson the Lord wanted to teach me was how to show compassion, forgiveness, and to stand in his ever-present faithfulness. Those traits are hard to follow through on in the workplace, especially when we feel we are being unfairly treated. But the Lord wanted me to walk with him in courage and allow him to bring about surprising results.

This would not be the last time I would need to stand

up with integrity. I regret not reporting the company, but as a young person fresh out of college, I was being advised by the temp agency to keep my mouth shut.

But I've learned over the years that when I stand up, the Lord is standing next to me. He has never let me down.

CHALLENGE

Have you experienced persecution or unfair treatment because of your integrity? Forgiveness is hard to give when you know you are right, especially when others would agree you have the right to be angry, to retaliate, and defend your honor.

Know that the Lord honors forgiveness and will not leave you to stand alone. But more than that, he blesses your life with his presence. He alone can change circumstances and bring about a happy ending. Are you willing to trust him, to believe he cares and is faithful?

Next time you have the opportunity, call on the Lord. Listen to his instruction. Wait for the steps he wants you to take. Then take them—one at a time.

Further Study

"'And then I will declare to them, 'I never knew you; DEPART FROM ME, YOU WHO PRACTICE LAWLESSNESS.' Therefore every one who hears these words of Mine, and acts upon them, may be compared to the wise man, who built his house upon the rock.'" Matthew 7:23 (NAS)

"'But whoever shall deny Me before men, I will also deny him before My Father who is in heaven. Do not think that I came to bring peace on the earth; I did not come to bring peace, but a sword.'"

Matthew 10:33 (NAS)

"'For whoever wishes to save his life shall lose it, but whoever loses his life for My sake, he is the one who will save it.'" Luke 9:24 (NAS)

Green Monster

"Fourteen days and I still have this flu. I've been running a fever of 102 or higher. Can't seem to shake it. I've opened the hide-a-bed in the living room. I'm trying to keep an eye on the kids. I'm wondering if you could watch them for me for a couple of days?"

My neighbors had the flu a few weeks earlier. I took their son and daughter in while they recovered. I had hoped they would do the same for me now.

"We had that flu. Bad stuff. We don't want to get it again. Besides, we can't get up to your house. The road is rutted out."

My heart sank. They were only a mile and a half down the road. I had helped them. They went to my friend's church. I thought for sure they would be open to watching the boys.

I hung up the phone and crawled back into the makeshift bed on the hideaway. Luke, five-years-old, was making French toast for himself and his brother. The electric grill made it fairly safe, and he had helped me many times. Nathan, 23 months, was piling colorful big Legos on the chair Luke was standing on. But his brother was not distracted from his job of getting them some breakfast.

Luke had used all his culinary arts over the last few days

to make grilled cheese sandwiches, pancakes and soup. To me, it didn't make much difference what meal it was; they were eating.

Two days passed. The torrent of the October rain was beating on our tin roof. It seemed the rain was never going to let up. I had bundled up a few days before, grabbed the wheel barrow and hauled firewood. The sticky red clay clung in globs to my rubber boots making it hard to maneuver the wheel barrow. I dreaded going out in the rain again, but wood was our only source of heat.

I prayed for strength to get up and get a few logs so we could keep the fire going. I was grateful that John had chopped wood before he headed out to sea for six weeks.

I'm not sure how much time passed. When I woke up, the boys were playing in the living room, and someone was pounding on our back door. Before I could rouse myself out of the hide-a-bed, the back door flung open. Standing in the doorway was a green monster. Or so he appeared.

"Sorry to just barge in, but I heard you were sick." The green monster was speaking.

He pulled the large green rain hat off his head. I recognized him as my young neighbor just down the hill from us. He owned 20 acres and stayed in a camp trailer on his place. His dark green raingear gleamed with water.

"Sorry to drip all over your floor." He didn't pause for a response. "I thought maybe you could use some help getting wood in."

He looked in the huge box we kept in the dining room. "Yep, looks like you only have a couple pieces left."

"I hauled a couple of days ago. How did you hear I was sick?" I queried.

"I was talking with our neighbors. They said you had the flu. I had it for over two weeks. Bad stuff! I thought you could use some help."

"Well, I have a wheel barrow out there, but the clay keeps sticking to the wheel and my boots."

"Ya, I know the mud is bad. I'll try not to track much into your house."

I thought, *Mud was the least of my problems!*

He gathered some wood and then came back. "Looks like the little board bridge you use to cross the ditch to get to the wood broke down. I fixed it for you."

"Thank you so much. We appreciate the wood."

"Oh, I'll be right back. I'm going to fill this box to overflowing. You should have enough to get you by until you feel better."

I didn't know what to say. To me, he was an answer to prayer, but as far as I knew, he didn't even attend church. I was grateful for his compassionate heart and prayed often that if he had boys, they would grow up to be just like him.

REFLECTION

I had been praying for help with a specific answer in mind. My neighbors, whom I had helped, were my obvious and expected solution. But God had a different plan; he had another neighbor in mind. That fall I learned to trust that God hears my prayers. I must not give up hope. And I need to remain open to whomever and however he wants to answer my request.

I have no idea what the Lord was doing in that young man's heart, but from my perspective, he knew how to put compassion into action.

CHALLENGE

What challenge in your life do you need help with right now? Have you been praying with a specific or expected solution in mind?

Praying with a solution in mind is praying with your eyes and ears closed. Keep an open mind to the surprising possibilities of what God has in his mind for you.

FURTHER STUDY

"'Come to me with your ears wide open. Listen, for the life of your soul is at stake. I am ready to make an everlasting covenant with you. I will give you all the mercies and unfailing love that I promised to David.'"

ISAIAH 55:3 (NLT)

"'Pay attention to Me, O My people; And give ear to Me, O My nation; And I will set My justice for a light of the peoples.'" ISAIAH 51: 4 (NAS)

"For thus says the LORD God of Israel, 'The bowl of flour shall not be exhausted, nor shall the jar of oil be empty, until the day that the LORD sends rain on the face of the earth.'" I KINGS 17:14 (NAS)

What Are You Afraid Of?

Reading a good book in the lobby of my doctor's office, I was interrupted as a patient rushed out the front door yelling, "Oh, no!"

My immediate thought was—the dog.

On my way into the office, I had greeted a forlorn looking collie. Tied to the fender of a bicycle, she stood at attention, watching the glass door through which the master had disappeared.

"They'll be back. It's OK," I reassured as I went into the building.

Sitting in the lobby, I watched the rush of commotion as the receptionist ran out the front door and repeated, "Oh, no!"

I tried to continue reading my book, minding my own business, but I couldn't. I got up to see for myself what all the fuss was about. Looking out the glass door, I could see the toppled bike and the leash in a tangled mess. The dog had slipped out of her collar. The owner was frantic. I turned to sit back down, but my heart was unsettled. I silently asked the Lord:

What can I do? I was not sure that I wanted to get involved. I really did not see how I could help.

The answer came quickly, *Go. Go help her look.*

Though it was unclear what I should do, I immediately obeyed and went out the door. The owner was still grappling with her bike. I silently inquired:

I don't know where to look. I don't know which way to go.

To the left. Go look to the left.

I walked past the building and onto the sidewalk; it led away from the busy street into a quiet neighborhood. As I turned to look down the sidewalk, there was a young man bent over, reaching for dog tags. I yelled down the street:

"Did you just find that dog?"

He looked up, shook his head "yes" and smiled.

"Well, hang onto her. Her owner is right here."

I took a few steps back toward the building and yelled,

"Your dog is over here!"

The owner gathered up the leash as best she could, put down the kickstand on the bike and turned to see her dog now standing beside me, along with the young man who found her.

She rushed to kneel down and give the dog a hug. As she talked softly to her dog, the young man and I disappeared.

REFLECTION

I could have minded my own business and stayed content reading my book. Even though I got up and involved myself in another's panic, I did not expect the Lord to direct me to the exact place the dog had wandered.

Just as he guided me then to find the dog, I know he is leading me now to a destination that is much longer than walking the length of a building. But it seems that I would rather sit and read a book than take the initiative to move into action.

While in prayer, I had been told three times to get my house in order; to clean up years of procrastination. Years of books, papers, notebooks that need to be organized, sorted or tossed.

It's not a job I like. Cleaning requires that I touch the past and reflect on the life that once was. Boy Scout hats complete with pins, ribbons, trophies, certificates of accomplishment, Taekwondo belts, pictures and a book dedicated to "the best Mom a kid could ever have."

I loved raising my boys. They are young men now. They are moving on with their lives.

I know that all of this cleaning, tossing, reorganizing is preparing me for the new life ahead: a first chapter of another novel of my life. This reorganizing is a way to accept change, to live in the present and affirm new roles.

What are you afraid of? the voice inside of me questions.
*I think…*I hesitate to answer. *I think my overriding fear is one of abandonment.*

17

A long pause—then I smile to realize—the dog—standing in front of the glass door—waiting—for her master to appear. Something frightened the dog and she ran off, but not far and the master came looking for her. They are reunited—with help.

"Oh," I yell, "I am the dog, and I need help!"

Oh, ye, of little faith. I am reassured. *Just as I take care of a stray and frightened dog, I will take care of you. I love you. I will take care of you just like the dog's owner loves and takes care of her dog. I asked you to help. I showed you where to look. As I care for them, I will care for you. Keep listening in the ordinariness of your day. I need you to stay alert. Keep your eyes and ears open!*

CHALLENGE

Do you stay conscious of the world around you in order to discover the messages you might find there?

You may be missing out, missing the stories in your life that give insight into the ways the Lord is trying to answer your prayers, insight into how an ordinary day can be changed by God.

God, more than anyone, knows the fears we struggle with. By keeping your eyes and ears open to the unexpected moments, you will find surprising ways God wants to guide your life.

Build prayer into your day. Not just at the beginning or end of your day, but throughout. Stay alert to the numerous ways God is trying to communicate with you. You may discover surprising answers to your own struggles and fears as God guides you through the crisis of another.

FURTHER STUDY

"Be strong and courageous! Do not be afraid of them! The LORD your God will go ahead of you. He will neither fail you nor forsake you."
DEUTERONOMY 31:6 (NLT)

"You have held my eyelids open; I am so troubled that I cannot speak. I have considered the days of old, the years of long ago. I will remember my song in the night; I will meditate with my heart; and my spirit ponders."
PSALM 77:4-6 (NAS)

"'Why are you afraid, you men of little faith?' Then He got up and rebuked the winds and the sea, and it became perfectly calm."
MATTHEW 8:26 (NAS)

"'…don't be afraid of those who want to kill you. They can only kill the body; they cannot do any more to you….Fear God, who has the power to kill people and then throw them into hell. What is the price of five sparrows? A couple of pennies? Yet God does not forget a single one of them. And the very hairs on your head are all numbered. So don't be afraid; you are more valuable to him than a whole flock of sparrows.'"
LUKE 12:4-7 (NLT)

You Have to Pray

"Diana, you have to pray for me."

"Why? What's the matter?"

"I've lost my badge. They told me that if I don't find it in seven days they will have to issue me a new one."

"Oh. How much does that cost?"

"It's not the cost. It will go into my file that I lost my badge!"

"Is this a big thing?" I was teasing her.

She smiled back and answered, "Yes!"

My boss knew I was referring to a conversation we had previously about prayer. In that conversation, she said she saved her prayers to God only for the big things. She believed she could handle most things without bothering God about them.

"You'll pray?" she asked again.

"Sure. I'll pray."

Satisfied that I meant it, she gave me a big grin and turned to go into her office. I wrote her request in the prayer journal that I kept at work. I prayed several times about it over the next couple of days. Then my boss's phone rang:

"Is this _____?" The voice on the other end was inquiring if my boss was in.

"No, this is her assistant. May I help you?"

"This is McDonald's. We have a badge here with her name on it. Someone told us if we called, someone would come pick it up."

"You found her badge?"

"Someone found it sitting on one of our tables and turned it in to the cashier."

Without saying anything to my boss, I left for lunch and headed to McDonald's. When she was done with her meetings that afternoon, I called her over to my desk:

"Remember when you asked me to pray that you'd find your badge?"

"Yes."

"Have you found it yet?" I asked.

"No and I only have a few days left."

"I've been praying about it," I told her.

"Good," she answered.

I pulled the badge from out of my desk drawer and dangled it by the neck cord.

"You found it!" She started to reach for it, but I pulled it back.

"Guess where it was?"

"I don't know. Where was it?"

"I picked it up from McDonald's."

"McDonald's? I haven't eaten there in years."

"Well, that's where it was. When I picked it up, the

manager said someone in the restaurant saw another person carrying the badge in their hand when they came in. It was pouring down rain outside. They got a napkin and wiped it off. It looked like it had mud all over it. They appeared to discuss the badge with the person they were with. The person who turned it in assumed they were trying to figure out what to do with it. They ended up leaving it on the table. The person who turned it into McDonald's recognized the logo on the badge because they know someone who works here. They told the manager that if they called, someone would come and pick it up."

"So you did."

"Yes. How do you suppose it got to McDonald's?" I asked out of curiosity.

"I'm not sure. I went to a funeral that day. It was pouring down rain. When I was leaving I threw on my coat. I must have knocked my badge loose somehow. I wonder if it floated down the gutter and landed in front of McDonald's. That makes sense because the funeral home is just up the street."

"I don't know. That's pretty fantastic! It seems to me there were a lot of people involved in getting your badge back. The Lord must have answered your prayers." I was grinning at her.

"Ya, ya. Just give me my badge."

REFLECTION

The unexpected loss of my boss's badge opened the door to tap into one of my highest strengths: prayer, a skill not often revered in the work place. But it was clear that prayer had surprisingly brought the badge from the gutter to the table, to the cashier to the restaurant manager, to me and then back in my boss's hands. Many people were involved in answering a prayer they were unaware of.

Being a part of building another's faith, watching the Lord work in their lives, even as they resist, is so much fun! God starts out small. He answers "the little things" in unusual ways. Eventually, friends, co-workers and casual acquaintances begin to see him working on bigger things. Their faith and trust grow. Want to know how I know? Because many mornings I was instructed by my other boss as she passed by, "Get in here!" She would shut the door, invite me to sit down, and then give me her prayer requests.

CHALLENGE

Being Christ in the workplace can seem difficult to near impossible. But when the Lord calls you to be courageous and step forward, will you believe he will give you the words and the timing to do as he asks?

Who in your life is the Lord calling you to be a prayer warrior for? Do they seem resistant?

Maybe when they were growing up they never had

anyone teach them how to pray. Maybe the Lord is calling you to be that person. How will you respond? Will you take a risk?

The Lord rewards those who seek him, who trust him. Take a risk. Let the Lord show you how he wants you to grow in him. You may never know or be able to anticipate the impact you have on another's life, but you will have *no* impact if you fail to respond.

FURTHER STUDY

"But I trust in you, O LORD; I say, 'You are my God.' My times are in your hands; deliver me from my enemies and from those who pursue me."
PSALM 31:14-15 (NIV)

"When I called, you answered me; you made me bold and stouthearted." PSALM 138:3 (NIV)

"…Give thanks to the Lord, call on His name. Make known His deeds among the peoples; Make them remember that His name is exalted."
ISAIAH 12:4 (NAS)

"Trust in the LORD forever, for in GOD the LORD, we have an everlasting Rock." ISAIAH 26:4 (NAS)

"'I assure you of this: If anyone acknowledges me publicly here on earth, I, the Son of Man, will openly acknowledge that person in the presence of God's angels. But if anyone denies me here on earth, I will deny that person before God's angels.'"
LUKE 12:8-9 (NLT)

What Trail?

Crawling out of bed to morning's light streaming through tall madrone trees, I saw a fawn and doe quietly munch on our late September garden. As I sipped on my hot cup of cider, I couldn't find the heart to chase them away from their gleanings. I watched as she taught her son to pay attention, to keep his ears up, always at the ready, as they enjoyed the last of my harvest.

I didn't have to wait long before my two-and-a-half-year-old son realized I was up. Luke was more interested in cuddling and reading a book than eating breakfast. Even though fall harvest and canning awaited me, I couldn't resist a morning snuggle. With John gone for the week, life took on a slower pace.

After spending the morning canning, I decided Luke and I should not miss out on the little bit of sun offered to us this time of year.

"You want to go for a walk with Mommy down to the mail box?"

His answer was short. He brought me his boots to lace up.

I didn't have to worry about unexpected cars speeding up the back road on our mile-and-a-half walk to the mailbox; even our four-wheel truck slipped in the red clay. I watched as Luke crawled into one of the ruts and began following the trail down.

"Not much mail today," I told him as I handed him a few

colorful advertisements to carry home. The breeze rustled the orange and yellow leaves that fall in late August. Luke ran after a few.

As we turned to head back up the road, I feared we had disturbed our neighbor's Great Dane. His bark echoed through the valley sending chills down my spine. This same dog bit our neighbor's son's friend. A rush to the hospital and nine stitches later ended their fun. They did not chain their guard dog, so I was not about to trust him.

"Come on, Luke. Let's go this way."

We abandoned the road, crossed a meadow, and headed up the hill behind our neighbor's house. I could not find a trail, so we blazed our own. Branches seemed to reach out and grab Luke's overalls. He tangled with the bushes a couple of times before I decided to carry him. Farther up the hill, the brush gave way to grass, and I was able to put him down.

Looking around, I realized we had found a meadow on top of the hill. The Cascade Mountains had started to blush with fall's brilliant fire.

Luke tugged on my leg, "Mommy, where are we?"

I looked around. I tried to get my bearings, but I did not recognize anything. I was so concerned about escaping the Great Dane that I had not paid any attention to where I was taking the two of us. I had no idea which way to go to get home.

"I'm not sure, Luke." Concerned, I thought, *If we were lost in the woods, no one would miss us for days. There would be no one at home wondering where we were.*

He mimicked me looking around, standing on tiptoes. I stifled a laugh. What good would standing on tiptoes do?

We were surrounded by trees and bushes that towered over him.

"Luke, I'm not sure where we are. Sit here, next to me. We need to pray to ask Jesus to help us."

I did not know what else to do. Luke nestled in next to me and bowed his head.

"Lord," I said out loud, "we need your help. We have no idea where we are. Thank you for protecting us from that dog. Now would you please help us find our way home?"

"Please, Jesus help us," Luke prayed in his sweetest "please and thank you" voice.

I looked at him, and he smiled at me. Then he jumped up and said, "I think we go this way, Mommy."

"What?"

"I think we take this trail right here. I think it will take us to the meadow by our house."

"What? What trail? I don't see any trail." I knew my two-and-a-half-year-old son had been in the woods with his father many times, but I was not as confident in his sense of direction as he seemed to be.

"Luke…" I started to argue, but I was not sure what to say.

"This way, Mommy."

Sure enough, there was a small deer trail! I was not sure why I didn't see it before. Maybe it was because I was spending too much time trying to see over the bushes.

Luke was already headed down the narrow deer path, so I followed him. I thought, *Well, maybe it will lead us to something I recognize.*

Luke strutted down the pathway ahead of me, confident

he knew where he was going. About ten minutes later, I could see it—the meadow just below our log cabin.

I couldn't believe it. Somehow I had over-shot the house and ended up on the other side of it.

Turning to look up at me Luke said, "See, Mommy. I told you." Then he bounded across the meadow toward our log cabin.

REFLECTION

I don't know what I expected when I prayed for directions. Perhaps an adult to come walking from somewhere in the woods, a spark of revelation, or, better still, the Lord's voice saying, "This is the way. Walk this way."

My two-and-a-half-year-old son taught me to receive answers in unexpected ways when I pray. As Luke grew older, it became obvious that he had a great sense of direction, but who would expect a two-year-old to know the way home? Only God.

CHALLENGE

The Lord teaches us, "*Unless you change and become like little children,*" unless you are willing to be humble and learn, as if you were a small child, you may remain lost and never find your way home.

Do you lose hope and become lost when you try your own direction? Do you find yourself wandering in circles?

The challenge is to keep your eyes and ears open. Watch for the unexpected ways God uses to encourage you to stay focused on him. Do you believe He sees with a much larger perspective?

When you feel lost, overwhelmed, and unsure of where to turn, he offers his Spirit, saying, *"This is the way; turn around and walk here."* Sometimes, you have to be open to accepting the messenger, not only the message.

FURTHER STUDY

"The reward of humility and the fear of the LORD are riches, honor and life." PROVERBS 22:4 (NAS)

"And the wolf will dwell with the lamb, and the leopard will lie down with the kid, and the calf and the young lion and the fatling together; and a little boy will lead them." ISAIAH 11:6 (NAS)

"'See that you do not despise one of these little ones, for I say to you, that their angels in heaven continually behold the face of My Father who is in heaven.'"
MATTHEW 18:10 (NIV)

Turn in Here

Have you ever had your doctor tell you to take an over-the-counter medication? Usually, he writes the name down and tells you where you can purchase it. But has he ever told you to buy a medication you have never heard of? Mine did. He told me I could pick up the medicine at a health food store.

Wanting to save myself time and gas, I tried looking the medication up online, but I could not find it. I called one of the health food stores my doctor recommended, but they had never heard of it. I was surprised and puzzled.

Not sure what to do, I thought, *I will have to run around and burn my gas in order to find it.*

I prayed and asked for the Lord's help. A few days later, I was headed to Newberg to pick up my mother to go shopping. I had two choices as to how to get to her house. This day, I felt prompted to take the route I do not usually drive. Crossing Hwy 99 on the road to her house, I heard the Lord urge me:

Turn in here.

I looked over to the right where there was a shopping mall.

What for? I'm already late.

See the Rite Aid? Go there.

They will not have the medication I need. The doctor said I have to get it at a health food store.

Go to Rite Aid.

I knew it was useless to argue. I turned into the parking lot. In my mind I was thinking, *I will go, but I will prove to you that I cannot get the medication here.*

I walked through the door and looked around to spot where the over-the-counter medications were.

Go ask the pharmacist. The Lord insisted.

I walked to the back of the store and stood at the counter. The pharmacist immediately greeted me with a broad smile:

"May I help you?"

"I was wondering if you could tell me where I might be able to get this medication."

She took the slip of paper from my hand, typed the word into her phone. "I can't see it."

"I tried. I could not find it either," I answered her.

"Wait," she said, as if concentrating on a crossword puzzle. After a moment of silence she said:

"See how he caps his letters, but not the first one. I'm wondering if that is not a small 'a,' but some other letter." She tried a few other versions of the word in her phone.

"Oh, yes, look. The first letter in not an 'a' at all, it is an open 'O,' that is not a line on a small 'a,' that is the second letter, an 'l.' So the first letter in not a small 'a,' it is a capital 'O' and the second letter is a capital 'L.'"

She looked the name of the medication up in her phone. "Yes, here it is. We don't carry it, but Whole Foods does. Here is a listing of their stores."

She helped me find the store near where my Mom and I would be shopping that day.

I walked out of the store—without the medication—but knowing exactly where to find it.

REFLECTION

Honestly, I don't know why I argue when the Lord gives me directions. Why is argument my first response? You'd think I'd learn.

I feel like Peter when Jesus told him to go back out and go fishing. Peter went, but I bet he thought, "I'm the fisherman. You're a carpenter. What do you know about fishing? I'll prove to you there are no fish in those waters today." Of course, the point is Peter did obey AND the Lord was right about the fish. (Luke 5:1-11)

Like Peter, I listened and obeyed even though it made no sense. The doctor had told me I would need to go to a health food store. I complied with God, but I complained that looking for it there was a waste of my time. I did not expect to find the medication at Rite Aid, but I would go just to prove I was right.

But as it turned out, the Lord did not have finding the medication in mind. He had knowledge I was not privy to. He knew the pharmacist would take the time to decipher the doctor's handwriting.

CHALLENGE

How often do you pray, ask for God's help, and then ignore him when he tries to give it? Do you argue that what he is telling you does not make sense?

Honestly, if you could make sense of something on your own, would you take the time to pray about it? So why, when God tries to help, as requested, do you argue as if all of a sudden you had better sight, better hearing, and could figure it out for yourself?

Obeying when prompted takes discipline and humility. Of course, you first have to be willing to hear, but then why would you pray and ask for help if you were not willing to listen? That would be like me going into the pharmacy, asking the pharmacist for help, and then walking away before she had a chance to answer my question.

Don't let pride keep you from listening and being obedient. True, it is hard when God answers your prayers in ways you do not expect. But resist trying to rationalize an answer.

Believe God loves answering in ways you do not expect. As any teacher, he loves the "aha moment" when you get it—he is Sovereign, you are not. In the process, if you are willing to deepen your trust in him, you will discover that his ways are far better than yours.

Further Study

"Hear my voice when I call, O LORD; be merciful to me and answer me."   PSALM 27:7 (NIV)

"I call with my heart; answer me, O LORD, and I will obey your decrees."   PSALM 119:145 (NIV)

"'For My thoughts are not your thoughts, nor are your ways My ways,' declares the LORD."
                                          ISAIAH 55:8 (NAS)

"'Master, we've worked hard all night and haven't caught anything. But because you say so, I will let down the nets.'"   LUKE 5:5 (NIV)

"'Friends, haven't you any fish?' 'No,' they answered. He said, 'Throw your net on the right side of the boat and you will find some.' When they did, they were unable to haul the net in because of the large number of fish."   JOHN 21:5-6 (NIV)

What Good is Prayer without Hard Work?

RRR…RRR…RRR…

"Can you rock her out?"

"I don't know. Let me see how deep she's sunk."

Our four-wheel-drive truck was stuck in the slippery red clay of our driveway again. I could hear the Oregon rain, beating down steadily on the cab of the truck.

"What's Daddy doing, Mommy? I can't see him."

In the woods there were no street lights to scare away the boogey man. It was pitch black. The fog was collecting on the headlights, adding to the eeriness of the night.

"It's alright, Luke. He's looking to see what we can use to put under the tires."

"Are we going to be stuck here all night?"

"No," I answered, smiling, but inside I wondered.

John climbed back into the cab. With an angry determination, he hit the accelerator again.

RRR…RRR…

Trying to rock her out of the grooves only seemed to sink her deeper in the mud. I sensed his frustration.

Slam! went the cab door. He was out in the pouring rain again, groping around for more debris to put under the tires.

The driveway had become rutted from the heavy October downpours. It was continually being washed away at the bottom of the steep hill that led to our log cabin. We had intended to put gravel on the roadway before the rains came again but—we had to choose. We decided we couldn't eat gravel.

I climbed out of the truck, went over to the side of the driveway where John was looking for dead limbs to stuff under the tires, and asked:

"Have you prayed about it?"

"No!" He resisted, and then he turned to give me a broad grin. We had just come from a meeting where we presented a talk on couples praying together.

"You want to pray about it?" I asked, encouraged by his smile.

"Sure...go ahead." I said a quick prayer, but it was obvious John was disgusted. I know that it wasn't that he didn't believe in the power of prayer. I remembered how several months earlier our pastor friend had prayed over this same vehicle.

—※—

At that time, our truck was loaded down with firewood. It made this horrible knocking sound when John pulled over to the boulevard near our friend's house. John was up under the hood getting ready to throw a wrench at it in defeat when our friend, across the street, asked "What's the matter?"

John, in frustration, told him about his "stupid" truck.

"Let's pray about it," our pastor neighbor encouraged, as he crossed the street to join John.

Now, John didn't want to insult him; still, anyone knows that you just have to figure out what's wrong, then fix it. But who could resist that smile of confidence? He bowed his head, and the pastor prayed.

When he was done praying, he told John, "Try it again."

"Now?" John asked. "But I haven't fixed it yet!"

"Try it."

Reluctantly, John climbed back into the cab to give it another try. He thought, "What a ridiculous waste of time. Anybody knows you pray over people, not mechanical equipment," but there was no arguing. He knew his pastor friend didn't know much about mechanics, but he was about to learn.

John turned the key over.

RRR...RRR...VAROOM!

Dang! It started! He thought to himself. *And there was no knock. How can that be?*

No reasonable explanation. It simply was gone, and he never heard it again.

—⚬—

Now in the October rain, the question was the same: "What good was prayer without hard work?" He would get it out, but it was going to take a lot of muscle...not just prayer.

"You and Luke go back up to the house. You might as well put him to bed. I'll get it out."

"Why don't you wait 'til morning?"

"I'll get it out! Go on."

I unbuckled Luke and lifted him out and onto the slippery mud. It was like slimy snot. We trudged toward the house. Red clay sticking to our boots made walking a greasy, cumbersome affair. I could detect the laboring four-wheel-drive behind us—wheels spinning, grinding deeper.

I thought back over similar nights. Sometimes the truck would sink so deep that the hubcaps would be buried. I could sense the rainfall washing my face as Luke's voice brought me back to the present:

"Mommy, what's that noise?"

"It's just a coyote, Luke. We're almost home. We'll get the fire going and get you warmed up."

When we reached our log cabin, it was chilly, but wood was waiting. Home was a welcome relief from the downpour. The beating rain echoed as it fell on our tin roof.

"Is Daddy coming, Mommy?"

I listened. "Yes!" Yes, I could distinguish the truck moaning up the hill. He had freed it once again!

REFLECTION

The test of time proves whether you will pray together or not when unexpected events catch you off guard. Years later, John and I have learned the value of joint prayer in good times and in bad.

Sometimes God helps us work through the challenges, other times he does most of the hard work. Either way, he gives encouragement and strength to keep going, to stay focused on him, and to take each day one at a time. He has taught us that he is Sovereign, and the more we trust him, the more he is willing to show himself powerful in difficult situations.

CHALLENGE

What about you? Do you pray when things get tough? It may be hard to pray with someone else, but praying with others is the glue that holds life together when things get tough.

Have you prayed and had unexplainable things happen? No reasonable explanation, except the Lord heard and answered with little effort on your part. Those are the times when you begin to understand the unconditional love of God. You overwhelmingly know he didn't require anything of you except humility and obedience. He does the rest.

FURTHER STUDY

"'Now go out where it is deeper and let down your nets, and you will catch many fish.' 'Master,' Simon replied, 'we worked hard all last night and didn't catch a thing. But if you say so, we'll try again.' And this time their nets were so full they began to tear!"

LUKE 5:4-6 (NLT)

"Simon Peter, '…I am going fishing.' … 'We will also come with you.' …that night they caught nothing. Jesus …said to them, 'Children, you do not have any fish, do you?' …'No.' …'Cast the net on the right-hand side of the boat, and you will find a catch.' They cast … they were not able to haul it in because of the great number of fish…the net was not torn."

JOHN 21:1-14 (NAS)

"'…go down to the lake and throw in a line. Open the mouth of the first fish you catch, and you will find a coin. Take the coin and pay the tax for both of us.'"

MATHEW 17:27 (NAS)

Four-Year-Old Wisdom

Starting like any other Sunday, I slipped into the prayer room before the service to join the intercessory prayer meeting. The only one there, huddled on an overstuffed chair, was a mom and her four-year-old son.

I could see that the Mom was worn out but had found a place of refuge from the Sunday morning bustle.

"Do you have a meeting in here?" she asked.

"I'm early," I said.

"We'll be gone. I'm teaching this morning," she added.

"What age?" I asked.

"Four-year-olds."

Making small talk, I shared: "I used to teach threes, fours, and fives . . . that was a long time ago." Then I asked the obvious, "You have someone to help you?"

"Normally, but this morning they are not able to make it," she replied.

Before I realized it, I said, "Do you want some help?"

"Yes!" she said, jumping at the chance to have another adult in the room. As I joined her in the classroom, I spotted a small boy at a table off by himself. The other children seemed to know each other and were excitedly chatting and playing. I sat down beside the little guy and looked at his picture, making small observations of his drawing.

"Is that your picture of God? He sure is huge. Look at all the wonderful bright colors you've used."

The boy did not verbally respond to my comments, but instead he answered by drawing what he imagined to be God's face.

After listening to the story of how Jesus healed a blind man, the children were instructed to make their own mini-books telling the story.

I sat beside my newly acquired friend and watched as he tried to decide where to place stickers in his book. He asked for instructions to be repeated. He wanted to be sure he was placing pictures where they needed to go.

"How do I cut these pages?" the boy asked me. He followed instructions well.

As I watched him engrossed in his work, I asked the Lord, *Why am I here this morning? Why am I missing church service to help in the four-year-old room? What is it you want me to see?*

My eyes were re-directed toward the little girl sitting next to my friend. She, too, was preoccupied by her work, totally oblivious to anyone around her. She had placed the stickers wherever she pleased sporadically on the story pages and was now cutting up the left-over stickers into a million tiny pieces.

Meanwhile, the little boy finished with his book and asked if he might make another for his brother who was sick. After giving him the materials needed, he set to work, this time thoroughly understanding the process.

When it came time for my friend to staple his books

together, I noticed the little girl was still cutting the stickers into pieces.

I said to myself, *OK, Lord, what do you want me to see?*

The Lord pointed out to me that the young girl was delighted with her task. She had learned a new skill—cutting paper. All the pieces she had cut were headed for the garbage. They had nothing to do with the task at hand, whereas in the amount of time given, the little boy had completed two books.

When my young friend's brother and mother arrived at the end of class, he was able to give his brother his labor of love and keep his own book. The little girl's mess was left behind and later thrown into the garbage.

The Lord seemed to ask me, *What made the difference?*

I went home and contemplated that question. More questions came to me:

How was it that the little boy was able to accomplish so much? Did he know how to put the book together?

I answered myself, *No.*

The little boy asked for help with what he did not understand. He checked back with me to make sure that he understood before acting. He diligently worked. Asking for clarification as he went enabled him not only to finish his project, but to repeat the process on his own.

The little girl, on the other hand, asked for no help, remained lost in her own world, and wandered totally and completely off task.

It was then that my eyes were open to see, *I was that little girl.*

The Lord had given me tasks to do, books to finish, and conferences to write. He had provided me with people to help, but I was caught in my own world—I had not asked for help. God wanted me to see that unless I was willing to learn an important lesson from an unexpected source—from a four-year-old—I would remain in my own self-made world—working hard, but accomplishing nothing. I would achieve just as much as that little girl cutting up sticky paper.

I could remain content, feeling in control while using my new found skill, like the little girl cutting up paper, but I would never move forward.

Or I could let go and allow others to be part of the process. I was being made aware that I could allow the skills the Lord had given me and others to bring projects to completion. He, in turn, would provide the direction, focus, and the continual help we needed to accomplish the tasks he had given.

REFLECTION

"God projects" take time, effort, skill, and a team. He provides the team. Through interacting with the little boy, God let me know that the team was right in front of me. What I needed was the courage and willingness to ask for their help.

The following week, after my "unplanned day" of learning from four-year-olds, I began openly asking for assistance. Friends and family were glad to support my efforts. Excitement generated as we watched plans move forward through our combined efforts.

My little friend did not just draw me a picture of God's image; he became an unexpected example of God's compassion and graciousness.

That Sunday the children had learned how Jesus healed a man born blind—the same lesson I would have heard from the pulpit that morning. It is a story I had heard many times before, but this Sunday God had a more surprising and specific message designed for me.

I came into the classroom expecting to help teach. Instead, God desired me to be the student. God wanted me to be willing to be helped and taught by someone much younger, less experienced, and less educated. He wanted me to learn from the wisdom of a four-year-old.

CHALLENGE

Has the Lord given you a task or a job, but you feel stuck because you lack the courage to admit you need help? God is the God of the impossible. He chooses to accomplish the impossible through community effort.

If the tasks you are doing can be done on your own, take a second look. Are you acting in God's will? Jesus worked in community. He called and formed the apostles. He allowed others to share in his work, to be a part of the effort to bring about God's vision.

Do you believe we are God's hands, that we are his feet? With others you can accomplish much. Like Jesus, you can finish the work your Father has sent you to do by bringing many hands together. Are you willing to surrender your control and allow others to help you move projects forward?

FURTHER STUDY

"And he passed in front of Moses, proclaiming, 'The LORD, the LORD, the compassionate and gracious God, slow to anger, abounding in love and faithfulness, maintaining love to thousands, and forgiving wickedness, rebellion and sin.'"

EXODUS 34:6-7 (NLT)

"'I tell you the truth, unless you change and become like little children, you will never enter the kingdom of heaven. Therefore, whoever humbles himself like this child is the greatest in the kingdom of heaven.'"

MATTHEW 18:3-4 (NIV)

"'My food is to do the will of him who sent me and to finish his work.'"   JOHN 4:34 (NIV)

"As Jesus was walking along, he saw a man who had been blind from birth. 'Teacher,' his disciples asked him, 'why was this man born blind? Was it a result of his own sins or those of his parents?'"

JOHN 9:1-2 (NLT)

"...lead a life worthy of your calling, for you have been called by God. Be humble and gentle. Be patient with each other, making allowance for each other's faults because of your love. Always keep yourselves united in the Holy Spirit, and bind yourselves together with peace. We are all one body, we have the same Spirit, and we have all been called to the same glorious future."
EPHESIANS 4:1-4 (NLT)

I Don't Have an Explanation

"How do you explain that, Lorna?" my mother asked.

"I don't know. All I know is when I woke up this morning my back didn't hurt, and my knee doesn't hurt either."

I could hear the clanging as the dishes were being taken out of the dishwasher and placed on the table for breakfast.

"Well, what do you mean it doesn't hurt?"

"It doesn't hurt."

"Well, how can that be?"

"I don't know, Dolores. All I know is that today it simply doesn't hurt. I don't have an explanation."

I could hear my aunt and my mother in the kitchen discussing the events of yesterday while I was staying incognito in the upstairs guest bedroom.

When we arrived the day before, my Auntie Lorna was complaining her back was aching and her knee was in a great deal of pain. My uncle emphasized the extent of her pain, "Yeah, she can't walk. We've been going down to the school to use the track since she had her heart attack, but now she can't walk."

I could see the look of concern on his face. Not being able to walk meant not getting the exercise her heart doctor insisted was necessary for recovery.

After dinner, we retired to the "other side," as my dad used to say, to watch some football. I can't say I was very interested in the game. I chose a spot next to my aunt and silently prayed over her knee.

John caught my eye. He pointed at the TV, shook his head as if to say, "This is not an appropriate time to be doing that."

But I smiled and looked the other way. What harm could it do? My aunt and uncle were unaware of what I was doing.

Then Auntie Lorna stopped her conversation with my mother to say, "That feels real good, Diana. Don't stop."

I knew she could not have seen John giving me the "stop that" look. She had been facing the other way. Now my mother became aware of what I was doing and gave looks of, "What are you doing?"

About 15 minutes later, my aunt said, "Oh, I'm getting so tired. I need to go to bed. My back is hurting. I'd better lay down."

As she got up from her Lazy Boy chair and started to walk away, I said, "Would you like me to pray over your back?"

She turned to look at me. "You know I'm not a believer."

"I know. Doesn't matter."

"I don't believe, Diana."

"I know. You go put your pajamas on. I'll pray over you while you lay down. You can call me when you're ready."

A few minutes later, she called me to come upstairs. She was settled into bed. She turned over, as I instructed, so I could place my hand on her back.

"You know I used to go to church, but ever since Debbie [her second child] was born, I don't go any more." She continued to explain the story I had heard many times. "Larry [her eldest] was in the hospital. He had meningitis. He was really sick. I was six months pregnant with Debbie. I was so worried about Larry."

I shook my head, "Yes, I know."

She continued, "I had Debbie early, you know. She was born with cerebral palsy. There was nothing anyone could do." She looked at me to make sure I was still listening.

She mentioned my hand on her back. "That feels good. It's almost like I'm under a heat lamp." Then she went back to her story.

"I'm not a believer, you know."

"I know. You must have been mad at God."

"Mad? No, I'd have to believe there was a God to be mad. I don't believe there is a God. I know you believe. But I don't."

"Yes, I do believe."

"Well, I don't believe."

"I know. He loves you anyway. It doesn't matter that you don't believe."

She turned to look at me as if to say, "How can you say that?"

I repeated it. "He loves you, Auntie Lorna. It doesn't matter that you don't believe. He doesn't require that you believe in order to love you."

She looked at me a bit confused and then said, "You know my sister died young. She was beautiful, a good person. If there was a God, I don't see how he could have let her die like that—an aneurism, so young."

She continued, "No, I don't believe there is a God. I appreciate what you are doing. The heat feels good, but I am getting really sleepy now."

I could see she was tired from the day's events, but I also knew that being sleepy is how others reacted when I prayed over them.

I kissed her, "Goodnight," and left her with her thoughts.

The next morning, I awoke to my aunt and my mother trying to make sense out of the fact that her back and her knee no longer hurt. My aunt convinced us that she was fine. She had no pain, and she would be able to join us in our walk around the school track.

REFLECTION

Many of us put God in a box. We believe he heals those who believe in him. But Scripture clearly says, "He died for *all*." Who are we to decide who he will heal, who he will not? We don't fully understand God. And the moment we claim that we do, he proves us wrong. He will not be dissected, categorized, and put conveniently in our scientific jar.

He defies explanation and our expectations of why,

when, and who he chooses to touch with his mercy and unconditional love.

While visiting with my aunt, she told stories of how the cerebral palsy children back in the 50's were wheeled around in children's toy wagons. She would not hear of it! She fought for Debbie. She fought for the other children to have child-sized wheel chairs, and she won.

She is a tower of strength and compassion. And some day, we will all understand why heartache, pain, and joy came into her life one April day in the 1950's, when her son was in the hospital with meningitis, and her new baby girl came into the world.

CHALLENGE

Have hard times hit your life? Have unexplainable things happened? Do you not know where to turn?

Sometimes we choose to turn away from the One who loves us the most. But his unconditional love is not affected by our emotions or behavior. He stays constant and faithful to those he loves.

If you have turned from God, will you gather the courage to trust him once again?

Surprising things may happen. You may discover the overwhelming unconditional love of God. It does not matter if you have turned from him. He has not turned from you.

Perhaps you have not turned from God. But are you tempted to put God in a box? Have you forgotten that he is Sovereign? Scripture says that his thoughts are completely different from ours, and his ways are higher than ours.

When you are tempted to forget, remember, he died for all. He loves and cares for all who claim not to believe in him. He is waiting for you, for them, to accept his love.

FURTHER STUDY

"The lamp of the LORD searches the spirit of a man, it searches out his inmost being." PROVERBS 20:27 (NIV)

"All a man's ways seem right to him, but the LORD weighs the heart." PROVERBS 21:2 (NIV)

"'My thoughts are completely different from yours,' says the LORD. 'And my ways are far beyond anything you could imagine. For just as the heavens are higher than the earth, so are my ways higher than your ways and my thoughts higher than your thoughts.'" ISAIAH 55:8-9 (NLT)

"But they do not know the thoughts of the Lord; they do not understand his plan..." MICAH 4:12 (NIV)

"Then Jesus prayed this prayer: 'O Father, Lord of heaven and earth, thank you for hiding the truth from those who think themselves so wise and clever, and for revealing it to the childlike. Yes, Father, it pleased you to do it this way!'" MATTHEW 11:25-26 (NLT)

"A vast crowd brought him the lame, blind, crippled, mute, and many others with physical difficulties, and they laid them before Jesus. And he healed them all." MATTHEW 15:30 (NLT)

"And the whole multitude sought to touch him: for there went virtue out of him, and healed them all."
LUKE 6:19 (KJV)

"'What is your name?' Jesus asked. 'Legion,' he replied—for the man was filled with many demons. ...."

"And they saw the man who had been possessed by demons sitting quietly at Jesus' feet clothed and sane."
LUKE 8:30-31; 35 (NLT)

"Then he spit on the ground, made mud with the saliva and smoothed the mud over the blind man's eyes..." (6)

"'Who healed you? What happened?'" (10)

"He told them, 'The man they call Jesus made mud and smoothed it over my eyes...'" (11)

"'Where is he now?' they asked. 'I don't know,' he replied...." (12)

"... 'Do you believe in the Son of Man?' The man answered, 'Who is he, sir, because I would like to.' 'You have seen him,' Jesus said, 'and he is speaking to you!' 'Yes, Lord,' the man said, 'I believe!' And he worshipped Jesus."   JOHN 9:6;10-12;35-38 (NLT)

He Awakens Me,
Morning by Morning

"Mommy, will you read to us?"

"No! Mommy's going to read to herself right now."

Luke put his head in front of my face to look at my book, "What does it say?"

"You wouldn't be interested."

"Yes, I would."

I sighed, "It says, 'Blessed are those who hunger and thirst for...'"

"I'm hungry!"

I continued, "'...righteousness, for they...'"

"Mommy, I'm hungry."

I continued, "'...shall be satisfied.'"

"Mommy! I'm hungry!"

"Alright!"

Read the Bible! God must be kidding. It was impossible! I looked at my schedule. I thought, *Maybe I can pray and read during the boys' afternoon naps.*

"Get back into your bed. I'm not done reading."

"But I'm thirsty. I want a drink."

"You just had lunch. Now be quiet."

"I'm thirsty…I want a drink."

We fought back and forth, and then I yelled, "Be quiet! I'm trying to pray and read my bible!"

Who was I fooling? I couldn't pray and read during the day. The fight for it was wearing me thin, so I tried at night.

This too was unpredictable. Meetings, children's, "I want…" "I want…" Even my husband seemed demanding. It was impossible.

I told God, *Maybe after Nathan* [my youngest] *was out of diapers and into school, we could become close friends.* The trouble was, I was starving for the words of Scripture and the Lord's company. I had to make time. But when?

I began to get up even earlier. This, too, felt like a joke. It seemed I was often up at least once during the night with the children. How could I possibly get up early? I know I had done it in the past before Nathan was born. Why was I having so much trouble now?

"Luke, go back to bed. It's not time to get up yet."

"You're up."

"Yes, but it's not time for *you* to be up."

"But…"

"Go back to bed!"

I laid down the law that Luke could not come out of his room before 7:00 am, and he was to be quiet. Then I prayed that the Lord would keep him asleep, because the morning was my last hope for time alone with God.

The Lord rewarded my determination. Eventually, I didn't need an alarm clock to wake me. I awoke automatically an hour before the others.

Easy? No. If you've had small children in your home then you know that sleep becomes one of the most precious commodities you can obtain. No, not easy, but the Lord seemed to be helping. The boys woke less and less during the night. Luke slept until 7:00 am, or he found some toy to play with until it was time to come out of his room.

Now, years later, the Lord wakens me morning by morning to come and be with him, but I'm not the only one.

—⚹—

I awoke one Saturday in January before dawn. I carefully rolled out of bed while John was still sleeping. I groped around in the dark for my housecoat and quietly shut the bedroom door behind me.

I love this time of the morning where life is still. It seemed unusually warm as I quietly walked to the kitchen to get a drink of water. I planned to settle into John's recliner, which we fondly call "the prayer chair." The house was dark, but the lights from the neighboring mill shone through the windows like night lights. As I rounded the corner to enter the living room, I noticed someone else already sitting in my favorite prayer spot.

"Hi Mom," came the voice in the dark. "Did you want to sit here?"

"No. No, that's alright. I'll go downstairs," I answered.

It was Luke. He was sitting crossed legged with his head bowed. He had returned from school back east and was starting his nursing degree while living with us.

Descending the stairs to our family room, I realized why it was unusually warm. Luke had risen early and stoked the fire. As I quieted myself into my second favorite spot next to the wood stove downstairs, I thought about the many times I fought for this precious time to sit and be alone with the Lord when Luke was little.

I began my prayer, *Thank you Lord that my son gets up early to be with you.*

REFLECTION

Little did I expect that my struggle to create disciplined time to pray was a fight for the benefit of the whole family. John began getting up early to pray by himself. We started praying as a family before the boys went to bed. John and I also prayed together after the boys were asleep. Though finding time with the Lord in those early years was difficult, it was worth it. My sons learned the value of being fed by Him.

Now that my son Luke is married, he rises early to be with the Lord before going to work. My youngest finds time after the others in his household are asleep. They both call home or email to ask for prayer. They know I will light a candle and remain vigilant until their crisis is over.

I don't know why I was surprised to learn my sons carried this discipline with them into adulthood. The added blessing is now my grandchildren have the benefit of parents and grandparents who pray with and for them.

CHALLENGE

Are you fighting for time with the Lord? Do you believe fighting for time is worth the effort?

You are not only being fed by God, but you are training your family—children, spouse, and those who visit your home—to value time with the Lord.

Do you realize prayer is the most precious skill you can give?

Scripture promises *"If you train up a child in the way he should go, even when he is old,* [even when he has hair on his chin at fifteen!], *he will not depart from it."* (Proverbs 22:6) Children learn what we teach them, especially when we did not know we were in a training session.

Be encouraged. Create time. Find your own space. Be prepared with a Bible, pen, and paper waiting. You will receive more than you were expecting—a family who seeks after the desires of the Lord's heart.

FURTHER STUDY

"Create in me a clean heart, O God, And renew a steadfast spirit within me. Do not cast me away from thy presence, and do not take thy Holy Spirit from me."
PSALM 51:10-11 (NAS)

"Train up a child in the way he should go, even when he is old he will not depart from it." PROVERBS 22:6 (NAS)

"He wakens me morning by morning, wakens my ear to listen like one being taught. The Sovereign LORD has opened my ears, and I have not been rebellious; I have not drawn back." ISAIAH 50:4 (NIV)

"For every one who partakes only of milk is not accustomed to the word of righteousness, for he is an infant. But solid food is for the mature, who because of practice have their senses trained to discern good and evil." HEBREWS 5:13-14 (NAS)

"All discipline for the moment seems not to be joyful, but sorrowful; yet to those who have been trained by it, afterwards it yields the peaceful fruit of righteousness." HEBREWS 12:11 (NAS)

But I Don't Want To

When John accepted a job in Arkansas, we moved from Oregon to unfamiliar surroundings. We temporarily rented a house until we knew the area. Our landlords had the house up for sale. One Saturday night, they called.

"We want to show the house this Sunday afternoon. Will you be home?"

The house was a wreck. The boys and I cleaned up the best we could that night and finished after we came home from church; then we left for the park.

When we returned, about 20 minutes before dark, the house lights were all on, and the front and back doors were wide open. My first thought, *Someone could be stealing our stuff!*

Then I worried about the electric and heating bill! When we entered the house, no one was there. In anger, I called my landlord:

"Whatever realtor you have showing the house, they are very irresponsible."

"What?" he questioned.

"Whoever showed the house this afternoon was very irresponsible. They left the lights on and the doors wide open."

"That was my wife and me," he answered.

I was shocked. I called thinking he would want to know and be concerned that the house had been left wide open. Instead, he was defensive and irritated. Immediately, he began to pick on the condition in which he found my bathroom.

"Oh, I see," I responded, "I unknowingly called you irresponsible, so you are coming back at me by de-grading my house cleaning ability."

Then he hung up!

His wife came over to apologize for his behavior. Then she said, "I clean my house on Sundays."

I explained, "We go to church on Sundays." We clearly had differing values on how to spend a Sunday.

"From now on," I told her, "I would appreciate more notice, as I clean my house on Mondays—after the weekend."

The following weekend at 7:30 am Sunday morning, the phone rang.

"We want to show the house at 11:00 am."

I went into a panic! Two of my boys' friends had spent the night, and again the house was a mess.

"We go to church on Sunday morning," I answered.

"That's OK. We have a key."

I had to make a choice. We went to church.

When we got back from church, they were there. The doors were again wide open. They were talking outside to the prospective buyers. I was hopping mad.

I sat down at my desk. I named what I was feeling:

contempt. I was so angry.

Right then and there, I looked up contempt in the dictionary*. It said, "The act or feeling of one who views something as mean, vile, or worthless."

Yes, I was thinking. *You are worth—less to me.*

The dictionary continued to give the definition for contempt, "To hold one in scorn."

"Scorn," I said aloud. I looked it up. "Scorn, deeming one as inferior or unworthy of our attention. Having contempt, passing adverse moral judgment on."

"Hmm…" I looked up adverse. It meant, "Turned toward the stem or main axis."

Then the light went on!

I had been doing a lot of "me" talk. "It's not fair to *me*! They should not come over and interfere with *my* life."

A voice within me said, *What are you afraid of?*

I paused to think.

Rejection…rejection that my landlord would hold my house in scorn…that he would view me as beneath him or inferior because of the way I cleaned my bathroom!

Again I heard within me, *What are your values?*

Hmm…I like to be accepted. I am afraid of being rejected, not because of who I am, but because of what I do.

After a bit of wrestling, I decided, I'm not going to change them, but I can change my attitude.

*Funk & Wagnalls, The Reader's Digest Great Encyclopedia Dictionary, 1971, Funk & Wagnalls Standard College Dictionary, Pleaseantville, NY

The Lord helped me to see, *They want to sell their house. They are under financial pressure. They bought a brand new house. Several times, Diana, they have hinted that they want you to buy their old house. You are a barrier to their need.*

Yes, I understood what that meant. We were useless to them, because we did not comply with their wishes.

Their old house was keeping them financially stressed out. Consequently, they were picking a fight with us. They held us in scorn, and I…responded in kind. My behavior reflected my attitude. They responded with the same negative attitude. We had become trapped in a circle of contempt, fueled by disgust.

I asked the Lord, *How am I to break the circle when I am so angry I could spit? After all, I'm right. They're wrong. I have a right to act this way. They started it. And they refuse to change after I explained to them we go to church on Sunday.*

The Lord helped me to see that until I could admit to my behavior in the situation, nothing would change.

My behavior? I thought.

Yes, you do not need to be swallowed up by someone else's anxious problems. Do the best you can, and then let it go.

*Hmm…*I thought. *I know the problem.* I wrestled for a while with my belief that they ought to be going to church on Sunday mornings—they ought to value church as I do. *After all,* I kept thinking, *I'm right. They're wrong. They should conform to my wishes.* I was sure God would agree with me.

But he didn't.

A defiant voice inside of me said, *But I don't want to. I*

wanted something to hit! I wanted to fight. I knew not to take my anger out on my kids. My landlords were the ones who deserved the full force of my anger.

I knew I needed to resolve the conflict either openly with them or within myself. After reviewing the situation, I decided they would not be very receptive, so I moved to resolve it within myself.

I changed what I could—my attitude. I detached from their problem of needing to sell their house and focused on my problem—a messy house.

I needed to consider changing my schedule. I began to clean my house on Fridays. I told myself, "If I were in their shoes, changing a cleaning schedule wouldn't seem like too much to ask."

REFLECTION

My anger led me to sit down and evaluate my feelings. When I prayed about the situation, I was surprised that God wanted me to deal with my behavior and my issues. He wanted me to realize that the change I wanted to see needed to start with me. I had to change my perspective. Put myself in their shoes. Be humble enough in him to make the effort.

It is natural to want someone else to change, to insist they follow your values and do things your way. It took strength to admit how I might be keeping the conflict going by insisting on "my rights."

When we bought a home and left the rented house, I knew I had done my best to keep their house clean and presentable for selling, just as I would have wanted someone to do for me. It was not their acceptance that I sought. It was a clear conscious before God that was more important. Some battles are best fought with that in mind.

CHALLENGE

What current situation has you stuck in anger? Have you taken the problem to God? Do you believe he will help you work through it? Or would you rather just handle it yourself?

Are you willing to make the effort necessary to resolve the conflict? Or will you insist on being "right"?

Just a word to the wise—God likes us to know he is Sovereign. He is in control. Your surrender to his will is the fastest way to receive the desires of your heart.

Don't miss out. Choose to ask him, listen for his wisdom, and then do what he asks. It is the way to the peace you seek.

FURTHER STUDY

"Depart from evil, and do good; seek peace, and pursue it."   PSALM 34:14 (NAS)

"An angry man stirs up strife, and a hot-tempered man abounds in transgression. A man's pride will bring him low, but a humble spirit will obtain honor."
                          PROVERBS 29:22-23 (NAS)

"'Blessed are the meek [humble], for they will be comforted.'"   MATTHEW 5:5 (NLT)

"'Blessed are the peacemakers, for they will be called sons [and daughters] of God.'"   MATTHEW 5:9 (NLT)

"'Salt is good; but if the salt becomes unsalty, with what will you make it salty again? Have salt in yourselves, and be at peace with one another.'"
                          MARK 9:50 (NAS)

"BE ANGRY, AND yet DO NOT SIN; do not let the sun go down on your anger, and do not give the devil an opportunity."   EPHESIANS 4:26-27 (NAS)

I Love You, Dad

Driving around Bend, Oregon was a great way of stalling. John, his brother, and I had volunteered for a task that had been avoided for months. In the car with us was John's Dad. He was relating one of his WWII stories:

"Now hear this, now hear this. This is the Captain speaking. I know that you have been wondering where our …ah…patrol…yes patrol area is going to be. Our orders are proceed to the South China Sea off Hainan."

"We were on the surface. I was on watch. We heard the Officer of the Deck holler, 'full left rudder, all ahead, flank, dive, dive, rig ship for silent running.'"

Dad had been a submariner during WWII. The events of those years were still vivid in his mind. He had told the stories for years, but now they were mixed together.

I had seen pictures of Dad in his Navy dress uniform. He was a handsome, dark-haired man. He wasn't very tall, but he made up for it with spunk. Also, he had a tender heart for women; with three younger sisters, he learned how to charm a woman.

At my niece's wedding he oozed with enchantment, as those who had been married the longest competed for the most romantic couple. Over fifty-five years of marriage had not dampened his joy for life. He "danced" with his wife as she sat in her wheel chair, circling around her, giving her a wink and a "come on woman, we've still got it" look. She giggled like a young school girl and blushed at his mischievousness. They were a picture of true love. I guess the 200 guests agreed. They won the award for being the most romantic couple.

As I sat in the back seat of the car, driving around Bend, I remembered the many events of Dad's life. He clearly had angels watching over him, including the time his ship arrived at Pearl Harbor—late, but just in time to miss the infamous bombing.

In recent years, I had prayed for him. He didn't frequent church, but he owned a dilapidated Bible his mother had given him just before he shipped off to join the Navy. I was concerned for his soul and whether I would see him again in heaven. The Lord clearly answered me by saying, *He has my heart.*

Indeed, he was a compassionate man. As a volunteer fireman, he had seen some action. He also taught CPR at the fire station.

Mark, John's brother, brought me back to the present as he addressed John.

"I think it's time."

"Now?" John indicated he would have just as soon kept driving.

"We can't keep driving around Bend all afternoon," Mark laughed.

"Got any ideas?" John mumbled to Mark. He was pretty sure Dad's hearing aides could not detect their conversation.

"No, not really. Do you?" Mark answered.

"No!" John half laughed.

"Well, we can't keep driving around hoping to come up with an idea," remarked Mark.

John knew his brother was right. They both seemed to hope the other would come up with some brilliant solution.

"What if he won't go?" John's voice expressed the concern we all had. "We can't exactly carry him in."

If John's Dad, who was sitting in the back seat with me, knew what they were talking about, he never let on. Instead, he continued telling his stories, seemingly unaware of their conversation. I started praying that the Lord would show us what to do.

"I know, but we got to do it sometime." Mark had the same concerns as John. Neither one of them wanted to go to the next step, but it was inevitable.

"O.K. Let's do this," John agreed reluctantly as he drove over to the memory care facility.

When we got to the parking lot, Mark went into action.

"You'll love this place, Dad. They've got great food, a big screen TV, and a garden to walk in. Let's go take a look."

But no smooth talking salesman was going to fool Dad. He knew where we were, and he knew he was not going in.

"No. I reckon I'll stay here. I'll wait here for you guys."

I caught the surprised look on my brother-in-law's face. I had never seen him speechless before.

But Mark was only stumped for a moment; somehow he managed to talk Dad out of the car, but Dad was not going to move away from the hood. He was enjoying the sunshine right where he was.

I had prayed while Mark and John discussed what we were going to do. The Lord prompted me to do as he had told me.

I walked around my brother-in-law, who was standing beside his dad. I stood in front of my father-in-law. I bent down so my eyes would be level with his. He looked at me like, "What do you want?" He definitely had his stubborn face on, and he was not going to budge.

We gazed into each other's eyes for a few moments, then I said, "I love you, Dad."

He blinked a couple times and then searched my face. I repeated, this time with more emphasis, "I love you, Dad."

He stared into my eyes, searched my face again, and then looked back at my eyes. He nodded his head "yes," gave a half grin, and dramatically offered me his arm.

He would walk into the building in his own style—with dignity and a woman on his arm.

REFLECTION

A year and a half later, Dad's memory had been deleted. He could no longer tell even parts of his favorite war stories. Dementia had taken its toll on his body. His mind no longer told him how to walk, eat, or recognize those he loved. He was in the final stages of life. When Steve, my other brother-in-law, took Mom to see Dad for the last time, he was silently laying on his bed. Steve asked her:

"How did you and Dad meet, Mom?" He had heard the story many times before, but he wanted to bring back happy memories for Mom at this dark hour.

"I went with my sister Gerry to a dance. I told her, 'Do you see that cute sailor over there?'"

"She looked around to where I was nodding and answered, 'Yes.'"

"'If he asks me to dance and wants to take me home, I'm going to let him.' Then he looked over my way and winked at me."

Just as Mom was telling the courtship story, Dad opened his eyes and winked at her. Then he drifted off to sleep.

"Did you see that? Did you? He winked at me. He heard me. He knows who I am."

"Yes, I know. I saw him," Steve answered.

And she started to cry.

CHALLENGE

It can be a hard transition to accept responsibility for our parents; to realize we have to make decisions for their lives. Praying and asking the Lord for his help was the only courageous way I could get through it.

Do you have some tough decisions ahead? Remember God will give you the words and the timing. Expect him to answer, because he will. He is just waiting for you to ask for his help.

Your courage to trust him with those most precious to you will hone your listening skills so that what is unexpected by others will become common place and obvious to you. We all knew we couldn't carry Dad into the memory care facility that day. But the Lord knew what Dad needed was assurance that we deeply loved him. In a way, it was too simple. But God's ways always are.

Who in your life needs to hear, "I love you"?

Further Study

"Honor your father and your mother, so that you may live long in the land the LORD your God is giving you."
EXODUS 20:12 (NIV)

"My son, be steadfast in honoring your father; do not grieve him as long as he lives. Even if his mind fails, be considerate of him; do not revile him because you are in your prime. Kindness to a father will not be forgotten; it will serve as a sin offering—it will take lasting root. In time of trouble it will be recalled to your advantage, like warmth upon frost it will melt away your sins."
SIRACH 3:12-15 (NJB)

"'By this all men will know that you are My disciples, if you have love for one another.'"   JOHN 13:35 (NAS)

"Beloved, let us love one another, for love is from God; and every one who loves is born of God and knows God."   1 JOHN 4:7 (NAS)

Fiber Optics

Headed out the door to celebrate our 41st anniversary on the coast, John and I noticed our get-away was blocked by a truck that had pulled up behind our packed vehicle. The driver climbed out of the truck and greeted us:

"You are the last paying customer in this area who needs to be switched over to fiber optics."

"Fiber what?" I said.

"Fiber optics. It has to do with fast internet." He saw the look on my face and quickly added, "It's free. We are putting it in all the houses in the area, and yours is the last one. I'm wondering when would be a good time."

"Well, we are leaving for the weekend."

After a little discussion, we agreed he would show up again on Monday. We took off for the coast.

That afternoon, while we sat on a log watching the white waves hit the beach, the Lord prompted me:

Ask John, "What is fiber optics?"

True to form, I argued, *Why should I ask him about that?*

You are missing an important lesson, Diana.

I thought about what the Lord said.

Yes, I had been in a hurry to get to the beach. I had seen the guy from the telephone company as an interruption and nothing else.

"John, what is fiber optics?"

He had some idea, but I didn't understand, and he was not sure how to explain it.

The following weekend my computer-savvy brother-in-law came to visit. I asked him to explain.

"Fiber optics is a lightening fast internet connection.

The old system is like cross talk on the radio. The wires within the casing can interfere with each other, so like static on the radio, you get interference with your internet lines.

With fiber optics, there are no wires; it is glass. Each strand of the fiber is as fine as a strand of your hair. Several are twisted together in a casing, but they cannot interfere with one another. Information is passed through the glass by light.

The light is not blocked by anything unless it is broken. The speed at which fiber optics is able to deliver information makes it deliverable in one whole piece.

So, you know how dial up comes in divided pieces, one at a time? Or with a slower internet it loads on to your computer screen, one small piece at a time?

I shook my head, "Yes."

"With fiber optics, it comes all at once. One whole picture. It downloads in a matter of seconds."

REFLECTION

So, what was the message? Why was the Lord so insistent that I pay attention? What did this everyday utility worker have to do with my relationship with God?

As I reflected, I realized God was using an unexpected means to teach me about hearing his voice. He was showing me that, at first, hearing his voice is like static on the radio station. I struggled to learn how to tune in. I had to overcome the interference of internal lies that block the reception between God and myself.

Once I became aware of the lies within, and diligently replaced them with the truth from God's word, I learned to fine-tune God's voice. In tuning in, I received His wisdom and learned to trust him.

The speed at which this wisdom is received often depends on me. I can break the communication by believing lies and turning away from God, but if I choose to surrender and focus my attention on God, then nothing can block the Holy Spirit.

It takes courage to surrender my control over situations and allow the Lord to speak truth, no matter how hard it is for me to accept. By staying attentive and not turning away, he gives me the ability to receive full pictures of information all at once.

God controls the fiber optic download. The information

is received in seconds. Yet, the inspiration that has occurred can take weeks and many words to explain.

CHALLENGE

Do you believe God wants to communicate with you? Do you pay attention when he breaks into your circumstances unexpectedly? Or do you allow the cares of your life to cloud your ability to hear?

You cannot anticipate when God will break into your world. The challenge is to stay focused on him, open and alert to how he wants to speak to you. If you allow the lies of the enemy to block your ability to connect with God, you are choosing to turn away from the very wisdom you need to guide your life.

Expect God to find surprising ways of imparting information to you. Be willing to stay alert to the creative ways he chooses to reveal himself. As you learn to pay attention, to listen in the most difficult times of your life, you will come to discover that inspirational fiber optic downloads are God's specialty.

FURTHER STUDY

"The Sovereign LORD has given me his words of wisdom, so that I know what to say to all these weary ones. Morning by morning he wakens me and opens my understanding to his will. The Sovereign LORD has spoken to me, and I have listened. I do not rebel or turn away."
ISAIAH 50:4-5 (NAS)

"I'm going to do what you tell me to do; don't ever walk off and leave me. How can a young person live a clean life? By carefully reading the map of your Word. I'm single-minded in pursuit of you; don't let me miss the road signs you've posted." PSALM 119:8-10 (MSG)

"In Him, you also, after listening to the message of truth, the gospel of your salvation—having also believed, you were sealed in Him with the Holy Spirit of promise, who is given as a pledge of our inheritance, with a view to the redemption of God's own possession, to the praise of his glory." EPHESIANS 1:13-14 (NAS)

You're That Woman!

The topic for George Fox University's Spring Women's Conference had been chosen—Getting Unstuck. The brochure said, "There are times in life when we feel stuck physically, emotionally, spiritually…"

Sounds like my book Undivided Heart, I said to myself.

Why don't you find out if the breakout speakers have been chosen?

I thought, *Was that the Lord's prompting, or was that me talking to myself?*

I wasn't sure, but it sounded like a good idea. I found the director's phone number and left her a voicemail. A few days later, she called me back:

"What makes you think your book would fit into our main speaker's topic?"

"My book is about becoming unstuck. It shows a person how to identify where they are at, how they are stuck, and how to get out." She seemed hesitant so I added:

"Do you know Dr. Breshears? He is one of the top theologians in the country. He has endorsed my book for the theology part."

"Gerry has endorsed your book?"

"Yes," I answered. Obviously, she knew him.

"And I know you know Virginia Philips."

"Yes, I know Virginia."

"She has endorsed it for the psychology piece."

"Gerry and Virginia have endorsed your book?"

"Yes."

"Say no more. We need to meet."

We chose a coffee shop near the George Fox University campus. When she arrived, we settled at a table away from the central noise.

"Show me your book," she said after a preliminary chit-chat.

"The best way to show you how *Undivided Heart* works is to flip back to the charts." I opened the book and proceeded to show her how each chart was connected to the next. She listened with attentiveness. After discussing some of my book's main points and telling her about how Gerry came to help me*, she said:

"I want it." She pulled a checkbook from her purse, and wrote out a check. Then, sitting back in her chair, she said, "Now that you have shown me the book I want you to tell me how it came about."

I looked at her like, "What do you mean?"

In answer she said, "Usually when someone writes a book like this there is something behind it; something that happened to make you write it."

"You mean what Gerry calls my 'road to Damascus' experience?"

"Yes, that's it. Tell me about that."

I told her of my ten day encounter with the Lord,

the inspiration of writing music and poetry. After that experience, I felt I was given the gift of hearing God at a different level. It was hard to explain. She did not interrupt. She leaned forward indicating that she was very interested. In response, I told her my first encounter with the ability to hear the Lord, a story called, "*Are You Alright?*" that I wrote later in my book, *Where is the Water?*

"Have you ever heard of _____?" She gave me a name of an author and speaker.

"Yes, she gave a retreat at George Fox a couple of years ago."

"Yes!" she visibly brightened.

"But who could afford to go? It was $400," I said.

"Yes, well there was that," she shrugged her shoulders and looked down.

"But I did go."

"You did?" her tone was curious as if to say, "Tell me more."

"I volunteered. I made the beds for the attendees." As I said this, her brows furrowed, and her eyes looked questioning.

I told her the story of how I came to be at the retreat and about the man I met there. In the middle of my story, I said, "The Lord had told him (the man), 'Go and sit on that grassy knoll.'" Before I could continue she sat back in her chair, raised her right hand, and starting pointing at me,

"You're that woman!"

And then she seemed to look at a scene behind me. I realized she was remembering something.

"Were you there?" I asked in surprise.

"Yes!" she returned her gaze to me. "I was there." She had a big smile on her face like she was seeing an old friend.

"Then you know all about his Scripture verse."

"Yes. I know the story," she assured. She signaled with a wave of her hand that I didn't need to tell her.

She said, "Well, that does it for sure. You are doing a breakout session."

REFLECTION

I find it fascinating how the Lord weaves the stories of our lives. I wonder how many people have actually been in the same room with us, have heard the same stories, experienced the same people, but we are somehow blind to each others' presence until later in life.

There was no way that I could have anticipated that the woman I had just met for coffee had also sat in a room full of people, several summers ago, listening to the same extraordinary story as I had.

It took courage to call her, to promote my book, and yet, little did I know we were not strangers. We had experienced an event together that had affected both our lives. It was obvious the Lord had set up our meeting in advance.

He knew it was not my contact with Gerry or Virginia

that would open her heart for me to do a breakout session at the women's conference. It was the fact that she had already met me.

My willingness to follow the Lord lead to connecting with the woman who would decide, "You are doing a breakout session." It was her curiosity and encouragement that lead to the writing of *Where is the Water?*

As I look back, I realize the story of how *Undivided Heart* came about started the summer of 1985, continued at Western Seminary as I sought Gerry's advice, and took shape as I volunteered at a retreat.

God was my networker, persistently providing opportunities to teach and sell my book in unforeseen ways. Trusting in His ability to provide lead me to meet with the Director of the women's conference and the privilege of doing a break out session at the college.

*(The reader can find the story of how Gerry Breshears came to help me with *Undivided Heart* in my book, *Where is the Water? The story is called *"Do You Have a Few Minutes?"*)

CHALLENGE

Are you able to look back and see the stories of your life woven together into a tapestry or rug? Keep in mind God can see both sides of the tapestry. He sees the side we see: the back where all the knots are; and he sees the front, a beautiful finished design.

Trusting in his promptings takes you on an adventure

planned long before you were born. Be confident he has the directions, as well as surprises waiting for you. When you are tempted to argue, to insist on your own way or go the opposite direction, remember you could mess up or change the perfect design: fulfilling the dreams he has put in your heart.

If you have already messed up or changed God's design, remember the unconditional love of God. He is forgiving and knows how to repair the damage. He is still willing to reveal his direction for your life. All you have to do is ask him to come and help you restore his plans.

Listen by sitting still and being ready to obey when he speaks. I will warn you, though: being willing to obey is not a one-time act. It creates a lifetime of seeking the extraordinary in the ordinary, requiring you to look for answers to your prayers in places you do not expect.

FURTHER STUDY

"You saw me before I was born. Every day of my life was recorded in your book. Every moment was laid out before a single day had passed." PSALM 139:16 (NLT)

"Seek the LORD while He may be found; Call upon Him while He is near." ISAIAH 55:6 (NAS)

"'So I say to you: Ask and it will be given to you; seek, and you will find; knock and the door will be opened to you. For everyone who asks receives; he who seeks finds; and to him who knocks, the door will be opened.'"
LUKE 11:9-10(NIV)

"And we know that God causes all things to work together for good to those who love God, to those who are called according to His purpose."

ROMANS 8:28 (NAS)

"Do you see what this means—all these pioneers who blazed the way, all these veterans cheering us on? [Reference to Hebrews 11, veterans of the faith] It means we'd better get on with it. Strip down, start running—and never quit! No extra spiritual fat, no parasitic sins. Keep your eyes on Jesus, who both began and finished this race we're in. Study how he did it. Because he never lost sight of where he was headed— that exhilarating finish in and with God—he could put up with anything along the way: Cross, shame, whatever. And now he's there, in the place of honor, right alongside God. When you find yourselves flagging in your faith, go over that story again, item by item, that long litany of hostility he plowed through. That will shoot adrenaline into your souls!"

HEBREWS 12:1-3 (MSG)

Winter Has Passed

When the Bible Study at our house ended for the evening, I walked the last person out onto the front porch. She turned and asked me:

"Do you know that you have a full blooming lily in your front flower bed?"

"Yes, I know. What's up with that?" I asked.

"I don't know. I've never seen that before. Lilies don't bloom in the dead of winter, much less in the snow. Truth is, they don't naturally bloom even at Easter. They bloom in late June or early July."

"I know. I know that's when they usually bloom in my yard."

As she walked away she was shaking her head, "I've never seen that before."

As I turned to go back into the house, I looked over at the white lily and asked,

What's up with that, Lord? Why is there a full blooming lily in my front yard—in the snow?!

The answer came: *The winter has passed, the snows are over and gone, the lily is in full bloom.*

I shrugged my shoulders as I looked over at the flower, "Yep, it's a full blooming lily, alright, and the snow is melting, but it's December." I didn't understand.

—m—

The following spring, I took a class at Western Seminary. My previous seminary advisor, Bev Hislop, was teaching it, and I enjoyed being in a group of ladies discussing a deep and fulfilling book. It was a great class, so I indicated:

"I wish I could meet this author."

My advisor said, "She's coming this summer. She is doing a retreat at George Fox University in Newberg."

"You're kidding," I responded.

"It's $400 for the three days," she added.

"I can't afford that," I answered, disappointed.

"Maybe you could volunteer. Here, I'll find the website for you. You could call them and find out."

I took the information and went home to pray about it. I felt the Lord was prompting me to call, to inquire, and to volunteer.

"We don't usually use volunteers," said the kind voice on the other end of the phone. "But I'll put your name on a list just in case."

Three weeks before the retreat, I prayed:

Lord, no one has called. I'm willing to do whatever you want me to do on this retreat. I'd really like to go.

Two or three days later the phone rang, "Are you still interested in volunteering?"

"Yes, I told the Lord I would do anything."

"Anything?" she sounded hopeful.

"Well, yes."

"It seems George Fox supplies the sheets for the beds, but they do not make the beds. Are you interested?"

"I said I would do anything."

"There are thirty beds—dorm room beds."

"I'll do it."

"OK. It's a win, win. You put the sheets on the beds. You stay and eat at your mother's in Newberg, and you get to go to the retreat."

When we got off the phone, I prayed to thank the Lord. He said:

When you make the beds, I want you to pray in each room. I will give you a Scripture verse for each person.

What do I write the Scripture verse on? A 3x5 card?

Marcia gave you embossed paper with a pink rose on it use those.

Yes, I remember my good friend Marcia gave me that paper years ago. Hmm…now to find it, Lord.

Preparing for the Retreat

TUESDAY

When I got to the campus, it was a hot summer's day. I checked in with the retreat assistant. She gave me a map and instructions on how to get to the two buildings being used to house the guests. She told me each room would have the sheets rolled up on the bed. After she handed me a master key and a diagram of the rooms, I headed for the first building and got to work. As I finished in one building and began to climb the stairs of the other, I noticed the retreat assistant was sitting on a bench enjoying the sunshine.

"Are you done with the beds yet?" she asked me.

"No, I'm just now going to the second building," I answered.

She seemed surprised that I was not done. She did not know that I was taking time to pray in each room. When I arrived in the first dorm room of the second building, I asked the Lord:

Do you think I could just write out the same verse for the remaining rooms? How about this short verse I used in the last room. It seems like a good verse for everyone.

No. They are individuals, and they each need a personal verse. Keep going. I will help you.

It was warm even in the dorms, and the beds were jammed between the wall and dresser drawers. I prayed for strength and the ability to hear each verse. When I was done making the beds, I returned the master key to the retreat assistant.

FIRST DAY OF RETREAT
WEDNESDAY

Sitting at the registration table, I helped the assistant direct people to their rooms and answered any questions the guests had. Most of the participants arrived a couple of hours before the first session. I watched as the assistant pulled an envelope with a dorm key in it from a box on the table. She handed the envelope to a man. He left to find his dorm room, but soon he returned:

"I don't have a Scripture verse."

"What?"

"Everyone is talking about their Scripture verse, but I don't have one. You see, I have to have a Scripture verse. My friend told me he would pray that the Lord would give me a Scripture verse on this retreat. So you see, I have to have one."

I was confused. I had given everyone a Scripture verse.

"What do you suppose happened?" asked the retreat assistant sitting beside me.

"I don't know." I was still trying to figure it out. "I put the Scriptures on everyone's pillows right after I prayed for each verse and made the beds."

"Made the beds," he echoed. "I made my own bed. My bed was not made."

Then I realized what happened. Even though I was given a master key to all the rooms, as I worked I had found the rooms to be unlocked with the bedding sitting on top of the bed ready to be made, as instructed. So, I did not keep a close eye on the room assignment diagram the retreat assistant had given me.

When I reached the second floor of the second building, I found two of the dorm room doors closed. When I tried to open one of them, it was locked. I tried the room across the hall from it, also locked. I was confused, because all the rooms so far had been open. I naturally thought these rooms were not going to be used for the retreat, so I proceeded to the other end of the hall. Adjacent to each other were two unlocked and opened rooms. I made those beds, prayed, and wrote out Scripture verses for each.

As I thought back over what had happened, I realized the man must have been given a key and a room assignment for one of the locked rooms.

"Here," the assistant said. "Here is the key to one of the rooms." The assistant randomly handed me a key to one of the open unused rooms on that man's floor.

When I got to the man's floor, which he had to himself, the doors to both unused rooms were still wide open. I entered one of them. No one had claimed the Scripture verse from either room. Then I had a second thought:

Lord, which room am I suppose to take the Scripture verse from to give to the man?

What is the number on your key? came the answer.

Looking at the key, I answered: *102.*

What room are you in?

I stepped back into the hallway to look at the number on the door post: *102.*

Must be the right room, came the answer. The tone of God's voice sounded like he was smiling.

Satisfied I had the right room, I grabbed the Scripture verse and ran back to the reception area. But the first session had already started, so I decided to wait until dinner to give him his Scripture. I found him waiting in line.

"Here. I grabbed this from one of the empty rooms," I said as I handed him the Scripture.

He took it from me and read it. Then he shrugged his

shoulders like it didn't mean anything to him. Later that night, after our evening session, he went and picked up the verse that had not been claimed. The verse said,

"I will be a Father to you, and you will be my sons and daughters, says the Lord Almighty." 2 Cor 6:18 (NIV)

SECOND DAY OF RETREAT
THURSDAY

On Thursday, the same man shared with me why he had come on retreat. He had lost his mother, father, a favorite uncle, and two other people who were close to him that year. Because of his job, he had not had a chance to grieve. His work sent him on this retreat, and another before, in order to give him some time to be alone with God.

That afternoon, we had time to ourselves to sleep, read, or to pray. During the afternoon, the man had entered his dorm room, sat on his bed, and looked outside. It was a beautiful sunny day. The Lord said to him:

Do you see that grassy knoll over there?

Yes, he answered.

I want you to go and sit out there.

Picking up his Bible, he headed outside into the bright June sunshine. In order to get to the grass, he had to cross over a decorative bridge that went over a small stream. As he crossed over, a famous verse from a Psalm came to him. He made himself comfortable on the grass and opened his Bible. He read from Psalm 42:1:

"As the deer pants for streams of water, so I long for you, O God."

As he continued reading the verses of the Psalm, he came to the verse I had given him,

"By day the LORD directs his love, at night his song is with me—a prayer to the God of your life!" Psalm 42:8 (NIV)

As he reread the verse, he realized that God had "gone out of his way" to make sure that it was God, alone, who had picked this verse for him.

Then the Lord said to him,

Diana gave you the right verse. You don't need me to be your father right now. You need me to be your God.

With the recent loss of his family, he expected the verse in Corinthians (2 Cor. 6:18) to be the verse he should have received originally, but the Lord knew he needed his all powerful God right now. (Psalm 42:8)

He sat and allowed himself to be comforted by the Lord.

In the evening, the man shared with us his afternoon. Later that night, at my mother's house, I prayed and thanked the Lord for His wisdom and direction in giving the man the right verse. In answer, he said:

I want you to eat breakfast at the retreat in the morning.

But Lord, I have been eating at Mom's. I…

Take your food with you. Be there for breakfast in the morning.

Last Day of Retreat

FRIDAY

After I sat down at a table in the cafeteria on campus, the man came up to me:

"Here, this is for you."

"What is it?" He handed me an 8½ x 11 piece of paper folded in fours.

"It's your Scripture verse," he answered as he stuck it under the side of my plate.

"My Scripture verse?" I questioned.

"Yes," he said as he walked away to get his buffet breakfast.

After breakfast, everyone headed out to the last session. I was busy busing my plate when the man again came up to me:

"Did you read it?"

"No, not yet."

"Well, read it."

"Now? Here?"

"Yes, read it."

I unfolded it and read,

"Come now, My love. My lovely one, come. For you, the winter has passed, the snows are over and gone, the flowers appear in the land, the season of joyful songs has come…"

Suddenly, I pictured myself the December before, standing on my front porch looking at the white lily surrounded by snow, when the Lord had said,

The winter has passed, the snows are over and gone, the lily is in full bloom...

Tears rolled down my checks. The Lord was confirming what he told me the winter before: *the hard times are over; your season of joy has come. I am with you always.*

"Yep, it's for you alright." Seeing my tears, he knew he had heard the Lord correctly.

At the end of the retreat, he told me:

"When I went back to my room last night, I told the Lord:

'*Everyone received a Scripture verse but Diana.'*

The Lord said, '*I gave it to you a few nights ago.'*

I said, '*You gave it to me?'*

He said, '*Yes, a couple of nights ago.'*"

"I thought the Scripture was for my wife. I wrote it down on the hotel letterhead. But the Lord told me it was for you. And when you cried I knew, 'Yep, it was for you.'"

He had no idea that past winter I had a full blooming lily in my front yard and that the Lord was preparing me for this retreat.

REFLECTION

I am used to being the messenger of the Lord. I am not used to receiving confirmation from the Lord through another messenger.

Before this retreat, I had just been through a difficult past six years of winter experiences, and I was discouraged because nothing God had promised me seemed to be happening. In those years, I had much to grieve over.

The Lord had called me to seminary, but shortly after I started, I had to quit my job due to health reasons. Two months later, I lost my Dad to cancer. Then my oldest son moved to Colorado and my youngest accepted a job in China. Throughout seminary, I was continually sick. My doctor advised me to quit, but I finished my MA. Then a recession hit, and my husband was out of work for a few months.

I struggled to see how God would fulfill the promises he made when he called me to "bind up the brokenhearted." Still battling with sickness, I finally began to work on the outline for *Undivided Heart*, but it was turning out to be a painstaking process.

I was disillusioned with how long it seemed to be taking. I had done nothing wrong; I was following obediently and patiently. God kept asking me, *"Do you believe I am faithful?"* I grappled to understand what it meant to have joy in him in the middle of such difficult circumstances.

The lily in my flowerbed in the dead of winter I knew was significant, but I had no idea that the Lord had spoken Scripture to me from Song of Songs. I had missed the message. The Scripture the man gave me was confirmation that the time had come to speak into people's lives through the books I was writing and the conferences and retreats I would be hosting. God was showing me that my time of waiting, my sorrows, my winter, was now over and had turned to spring. The joy I had struggled to find, I finally understood, could only be found in Him alone; finding joy wasn't dependent on my circumstances.

I was grateful for this man's heart. He could have taken his verses and spent his time at the retreat receiving comfort from the Lord in his grief. But instead he asked, "What can I do? What Scripture of comfort can I give?" He could have persisted that the verses given to him were a gift for his wife, to encourage and comfort her in their loss, but instead he chose to listen to the Lord and release the gift to a total stranger.

God has called me to comfort the broken-hearted. But the man showed me that it is the broken-hearted who give "*… Liberty to captives and proclaim the favorable year of the Lord.*"— freedom to follow Him wherever he leads.

CHALLENGE

When the Lord calls you to do something out of the ordinary, when he entrusts you with a message for someone else, do you obey? Or do you argue and make excuses of why it is not convenient? While you are waiting on the Lord for change, are you open to helping others? Or do you stubbornly refuse to help until God helps you first?

Binding up the broken-hearted, while in your own pain, gives you the opportunity to reach out from a place of understanding. Being a blessing to others in your time of sorrow opens you to receive comfort from God. You will begin to experience the joy of God's presence and come to understand what it means to be "pure of heart."

Would you be willing to receive a message from a complete stranger who seemed to understand your pain? Or would you ignore it? Just as the man discovered, it is important that you humbly listen and believe God to provide what you need, not when/how/what you think you need. Recognize God's sovereignty, just as this man did, in the middle of your winters.

Don't be afraid to follow through and obey God when he asks you to do something big or small, unexpected or out of your element, like giving a stranger a scripture verse or making the beds at a retreat. You can never anticipate how much a message from God can impact another person's life or what blessings God has in store for you if you are obedient to him. When I asked the man if I might publish our story, he said, "This is so amazing to me and such an honor that God used me in this way in your life. I had no idea."

He was just as surprised at how much the message meant to me as I was to see a lily in the snow in the dead of winter. God-ordained events change lives. We need to stay alert to these extraordinary moments in the ordinary. If we do, if we are willing to humble ourselves, in the middle of our winters of sorrows and struggles God will provide us with the power to turn our own and others' winters into springs.

FURTHER STUDY

"As the deer pants for the water brooks, so my soul pants for You, O God. My soul thirsts for God, for the living God; When shall I come and appear before God? My tears have been my food day and night, while they say to me all day long, 'Where is your God?'"

PSALM 42:1-3 (NAS)

"Come now, My love. My lovely one, come. For you, the winter has passed, the snows are over and gone, the flowers appear in the land, the season of joyful songs has come. The cooing of the turtledove is heard in our land. Come now, My love. My lovely one, come. Let me see your face and let Me hear your voice, for your voice is sweet and your face is beautiful. Come now, My love. My lovely one, come." SONG OF SONGS 2:10-14

"Then I heard the voice of the Lord, saying, 'Whom shall I send, and who will go for Us?' Then I said, 'Here am I. Send me!'" ISAIAH 6:8 (NAS)

"He has sent me to bind up the brokenhearted, to proclaim liberty to captives, and freedom to prisoners; to proclaim the favorable year of the Lord."

ISAIAH 61:1-2 (NAS)

"Dry bones, hear the word of the LORD! This is what the Sovereign LORD says to these bones: 'I will attach tendons to you and make flesh come upon you and cover you with skin; I will put breath in you, and you will come to life. Then you will know that I am the LORD.'" Ezekiel 37:4-6 (NIV)

"'Blessed are those who mourn, for they will be comforted…Blessed are the pure in heart, for they will see God.'" Matthew 5:4, 8 (NIV)

"…and he fell to the ground, and heard a voice saying to him, 'Saul, Saul, why are you persecuting Me?' And he said, 'Who are You, Lord?' And He said, 'I am Jesus whom you are persecuting, but get up, and enter the city, and it will be told you what you must do…' And immediately there fell from his eyes something like scales, and he regained his sight, and he got up and was baptized. And he took food and was strengthened." ACTS 9:4, 18-19 (NAS)

115

Want an Intimate Relationship with God?

 Where is the Water? invites you to train yourself to hear God's voice and open your eyes to his presence. He desires to be known. He longs to share his love. Acquire renewed faith, hope, and confidence that God can and will transform your ordinary days into extraordinary ones.

 *Undivided Heart* - Book One
Bridging My Relationship with Myself, Others, and God
Discover the personal stories or events in your life that have you stuck emotionally and spiritually. Expose the four lies that hold you back from an intimate relationship with God. Gain a new perspective. Take action. Equip yourself with the eight truths which will help you live a new life filled with joy!

 Undivided Heart - Book Two
Bridging My Relationship with Myself, Others, and God

Learn the five levels of communication that enhance or hinder your relationships. Let God heal the wounds of your past caused by betrayal, humiliation, abandonment or alienation. Gain the power that enables you to love yourself and others.

For books, blog, or to schedule Diana Greene to speak at a conference, retreat, or seminar, please visit **www.dianagreeneministries.com**

Diana Greene Ministries, LLC, PO Box 902, Molalla, OR 97038

"Diana's love for Jesus and long journey of a deep personal walk with Him gave her the wealth of experience to integrate many facets of spiritual formation into a course of study and a work book that enables people to find what divides their hearts, minds, and emotions."

Gerry Breshears, PhD, Professor of Theology
Western Seminary, Portland, OR
Co-Author of *Death by Love*

"Diana has written an excellent in-depth study beneficial to all who work through the materials. *Undivided Heart* is founded on Biblical principles as well as psychological and relational insight. I would encourage individuals to complete this study as they will find it constructive for healing and growth."

Norm Thiesen, PhD, Professor of Pastoral Counseling
Western Seminary, Portland, OR

"I found the manuscript to be inspired by the Holy Spirit and done in excellence. I believe it will inspire those who are blessed to participate in her teaching. I was certainly encouraged when I read it. It is so timely and introspective. It promotes personal growth and healing in emotions as one experiences the heart of God."

Virginia Phillips, PhD, Founder & President
Women of Purpose, International
Author of *Heart to Heart Connection*

"Diana Greene's material in *Undivided Heart* is not only Biblical, it is powerfully effective. I know, it has helped change my life. I have seen wonderful changes in how I view and respond to God, myself, and others. The impact has been so significant that I find myself repeating the information on a regular basis to others. I strongly encourage you to allow the truth that Diana has written to encourage, heal, and strengthen your life."

Dr. Vance Hardisty, DMin, President of Renewal International
Author/Host of the *Patriot and Preacher Show*

PRAISE FOR *Undivided Heart*

"Through scripture, Diana taught us how to move from fear to courage, from confusion to peace, from a feeling of being unloved to acceptance, from hopelessness and depression to joy and fulfillment. I was able to identify the lies I believed and begin renewing my mind with the truth of God's Word. I strongly recommend the class. It will change your life as it has changed mine."

Barbara Baker, Mother, Grandmother
Office worker, Pastor's wife

"God has used Diana in a powerful way in my life to lead me through the swirling waters of transitions into a deeper and more profound walk with him. Diana has a unique combination of gifts. She has the ability to hear and listen to God's voice as she's counseling women. She asks questions that help dig into the root of a problem rather than just the surface issues. She also has seminary training which enables her to guide women through crisis. I truly do not know where I'd be in my walk with the Lord if God had not brought her into my life."

Julie Hardisty, Attorney at Law, Pleasant Hill, CA

"I am full of praise and gratefulness for God using Diana to speak into my life's journey. I have had great success using her charts to make life decisions."

JoAnn Harper, Office Manager, OR

"I'm breaking down my personal barriers in God's path for me…..During the class, the integration of physical, mental, emotional, and spiritual exercises revealed deficits in these four areas, and then highlighted corrective actions for eliminating problem behaviors."

Claire Cunningham, BS
Speech Pathologist Assistant, Roseburg, OR

"Diana Greene's book of prayer parables is a delightful journey that will take the reflective reader deep into prayer, the life blood of our relation with Jesus. Drink deeply and grow."

Gerry Breshears, Professor of Theology
Western Seminary, Portland, OR
Co-Author of *Death by Love*

"Diana Greene's journey with the Lord draws you into a desire for more: more listening, more attending, and more awareness of how close our Lord Jesus really is to each of us. Take time to let the water soak into your soul. Drink deep. Remain in his presence. He really does care for you. You can't miss that message in *Where is the Water?*"

Bev Hislop
Assoc. Professor of Pastoral Care to Women
Western Seminary, Portland, OR
Author of *Sherpherding a Woman's Heart*

"Unplug our ears, Lord. We long to hear Your voice. Use Diana Greene's book to pole vault our prayers over the mediocre monologues and toward dialogues with the Divine."

Judy Squier, Speaker
Author of *His Majesty in Brokenness*

"I purchased *Where is the Water?* for a cousin, and she wrote me the following note: 'Thank you for the short stories from Diana Greene. Her experiences touch the depth of the heart and leave you feeling moved by the Holy Spirit.'"

Amber M. Guillen, Co-Owner and Accountant
Book Entry Tech, Oregon City, OR

PRAISE FOR WHERE IS THE WATER?

"I LOVE Diana's new book—wonderful and inspiring!!"
Andrea Premazzi-Bauer, ND, LMT

"I just finished Diana's latest book. It encourages me to believe
that the Lord really is involved in my ordinary life, as He is in
yours. Thanks so much for writing it, Diana! You are a gifted
writer and speaker."

Annie Lawrie
Staff for Women's Ministries
Cascade Bible, Portland, OR

"Each story in *Where is the Water?* reignited my heart with a
hunger and desire to hear the voice of God in my own life
stories. It is evident Diana's heart is intimately tuned to hear
God and experience His presence in the "daily-ness" of life.
Come. Reflect. Listen. Learn how to abundantly receive the
everlasting water!"

Sue Hazen, Office Manager and Pastor's wife

"When preparing for a particularly stressful medical test, I
picked up *Where is the Water?*. I found the quote, 'I sought
the LORD, and he answered me; he delivered me from all my
fears.' I said to myself: remember I'm not doing this alone, I can
ask for help, and He will be there. During the test, I visualized
Jesus standing beside me as we looked out over the ocean. I
knew I was not alone, and I was not afraid; I found peace in the
message in this book."

Kier Hartwig, Hospice Volunteer
and retired Accounting Comptroller